ANCIENT S

of the

FOUNTAIN

of

YOUTH

BOOK 2

ANCIENT SECRET

of the

FOUNTAIN

of

YOUTH

BOOK 2

A companion to the book by Peter Kelder

HARBOR PRESS

GIG HARBOR, WASHINGTON

ANCIENT SECRET OF THE FOUNTAIN OF YOUTH, BOOK 2

Copyright ©1999 by Harbor Press, Inc.

ISBN 0-936197-31-5

Printed in the United States of America

10 9 8 7 6 5 4 3 2 1

Harbor Press, Inc.
P.O. Box 1656
Gig Harbor, WA 98335

To Peter Kelder

*on behalf of those who have
gratefully received this gift*

CONTENTS

F O R E W O R D

In this volume, you will be introduced to ideas, techniques, and wisdom that can empower you, enhance your health, increase your joy of living, and cause you to live longer. However, you won't notice that you're living longer. You'll be too busy enjoying life and living it fully.

I often see people start to live their lives to the fullest only after they develop a life-threatening illness and must come to grips with their own mortality. When this happens, they experience a spiritual and physical rebirth so powerful it can improve or even cure the illness completely. Once this renewal process takes over, aging ends and youthing begins. Please, don't wait until you're facing death to set the youthing process in motion in your life. Begin it now.

This book is intended to help you do just that. In it, you'll discover a wonderful series of simple exercises called the Five Rites. You will also find a wealth of related information on diet, breathing, voice energetics, and many other topics. You will read about the uplifting experiences of people who practice the Five Rites. And you'll find advice and insights from physicians who will share their knowledge with you.

But as you read the pages that follow, keep in mind that this book is not really about ritual, or exercise, or techniques. At its heart, it is about you — your uniqueness, your attitudes and beliefs, your desires and hopes, your potential, your ability to joyfully embrace life and live it fully.

Science has demonstrated that your body and brain are physically altered by both your activities and your thoughts. By the same token, you can purposefully alter your activities and thoughts to achieve your goals for change. The exercises and techniques in this book are aimed at this very thing. I have done the Five Rites, and they make a lot of sense to me. I am convinced that if you do them regularly, and if you engage in life joyfully, you will improve your physical health and your mental outlook, and you will begin the youthing process.

Also, you will access and put to use the life force energy which is the essence of all things. Science now has the ability to measure this energy and is beginning to explore it. I have experimented with this book's advice on mantras and mantrums, and I can feel the energy difference they make. Allow me to share this story:

The other night I was meditating and performing my mantras while lying in bed. My cats were in bed with me, curling up to go to sleep. My wife, who was in the other room, could feel an unusual energy, and she came in to see what was happening. When she entered, I opened my eyes and discovered that the cats had also sensed something unusual. They were sitting upright, as alert and wide awake as I have ever seen them at 11 p.m.. To me, the incident demonstrated how real and palpable this energy is and how it can make things happen in your life, things that are sensed and perceived by those around us.

My advice to you is this: Take the valuable information you are about to read. Bring to it your own insights and inspiration. Then, create your own personal transformation. Remember, you will not find the fountain of youth by looking outside yourself. The source of all things is found by going within.

So start right now!

Peace,
Bernie S. Siegel, M.D.

P U B L I S H E R ' S
I N T R O D U C T I O N

When the last key had made its imprint, he pushed back from his typewriter, made a neat pile of the pages he had written, and gazed with mixed satisfaction and uncertainty at the title page which read, "*The Eye of Revelation* by Peter Kelder."

The manuscript which Kelder held in his hands was not a major literary feat. But it was well crafted, short, simple, and direct. Moreover, it conveyed a message which many have since found meaningful and even profound. Even so, Kelder could not have imagined then, in 1939, that his little book would endure for generations, to be read by millions of people throughout the world in a dozen languages and even in braille.

His book told the story of five ancient Tibetan exercises brought to the West by a retired British Army officer identified only as Colonel Bradford. The Five Rites, as they were called, were said to unlock the secret of nothing less than the fabled fountain of youth.

Kelder's book was published soon thereafter, and while it was not a best-seller, it was popular enough to be expanded and reissued eight years later in 1947. Even when it did eventually go out of print, it showed surprising staying power. Kelder's book survived by word-of-mouth as copies were passed from hand to hand, and in time it gained the status of a cult classic.

Then, in 1985 Kelder updated his book and it was republished by Harbor Press under the title *Ancient Secret of the Fountain of Youth*. By then, more than half a century had elapsed since the book initially appeared, and the world was a very different place. Western culture, coming to terms with a new age of technology, had begun to search for answers in the ancient wisdom of the East. Eastern mysticism, the concept of subtle energy, the practice of yoga, and the belief that these things interacted with health and physical aging, were no longer the odd concepts of a lunatic fringe. They had become fixtures of Western popular culture.

Destiny had finally caught up with Peter Kelder's small book. Promoted only by word-of-mouth, it caught on, slowly at first, and then with gathering momentum. Within ten years *Ancient Secret of the Fountain of Youth* became an international publishing phenomenon. In the U.S., it outsold many *New York Times* best-sellers. In Germany, Austria, and Switzerland the book became virtually a national institution. It remains on the German language best-seller lists today, a decade after it was first published. And two dozen foreign language editions have spread the popularity of Kelder's book throughout the world.

Of course, Peter Kelder's book could not have enjoyed such huge success if it had not made good on its fundamental promise: to help the reader achieve renewed youth, health, and vitality. Certainly that conclusion is supported by the deluge of mail readers have sent to the publisher for more than ten years. Their letters tell how the Five Rites have benefited them in ways ranging from modest to miraculous.

Aside from passing on their stories of personal success, letters from readers have frequently asked two things. First, they want more detailed information on a variety of topics discussed fleetingly in Kelder's brief original volume. Second, they want to know more about the book's mysterious author, not to mention his leading character, the elusive Colonel Bradford.

The book you now hold in your hands has been written in response to the first of these inquiries. *Ancient Secret of the Fountain of Youth, Book 2* contains a wealth of information which picks up where Kelder's original (now renamed *Ancient Secret of the Fountain of Youth, Book 1*) leaves off. Each chapter of the book is written by an expert on the topic at hand.

Chapter One summarizes the story of Colonel Bradford and his Tibetan expedition for those unfamiliar with *Book 1*.

Chapter Two looks to the historical record to answer the question, Was Colonel Bradford's far-fetched tale of Tibet fact or fiction? Either way, it concludes, Bradford's story could well have happened, for numerous, well-documented accounts brought back by early Tibetan travelers record magic and mystery no less incredible than that witnessed by Bradford.

Chapter Three validates the Five Rites through remarkable, real-life stories told by people who have benefited from them.

Chapter Four probes the energy secrets of the Five Rites in an attempt to answer the question, What enables these simple exercises to perform their magic?

Chapter Five looks at the Five Rites from the perspective of a medical doctor who is also a yoga expert. It discusses the exercises in detail and supplements them with an abundance of helpful advice.

Chapters Six and Seven discuss two topics briefly visited in *Book 1:* the health benefits of proper diet and food combining, and the energetics of the voice, sound, and meditation.

Chapter Eight concludes with insights from one of the world's foremost Tibetan scholars. Dr. Robert Thurman gives an overview of the Five Rites *vis-à-vis* Tibet's history and culture.

And now for the second topic which readers have inquired

about: Kelder and Bradford. For years readers have written the publisher with questions about these two, whom, they assume, are no longer living. This is something which amuses Kelder, for yes, he is alive and well today more than half a century after the publication of his book. I am pleased to report that I personally know him and count him as a close and trusted friend, though there are many things I do not know about him.

Unfortunately, most must remain just that, for Kelder is determined not to disturb the veil of mystery that intrigues me and so many others. He is an intensely private and unassuming man who believes that the words he has written speak for themselves. And he maintains that extraneous issues concerning himself and Bradford can serve only to distract from the validity of the simple, straightforward message which he has put before the world.

To be sure, I have no wish to intrude upon Kelder's privacy. Yet I do understand the desire of readers to feel more closely connected to a man whose words have so greatly influenced, even transformed their lives. So, I trust he will forgive me if I do now for the first time select a few details about his life and pass them on to the reader.

Kelder was raised by loving, adoptive Dutch parents in the midwestern United States, and while still a teenager, he left home with their consent to undertake life's challenges. Later, Kelder, like Colonel Bradford, "traveled to virtually every corner of the globe" as an officer in the merchant marine. He became a polished, articulate, and learned man conversant in many languages, and throughout his life he maintained a love of books and libraries, words and poetry.

On a memorable spring morning not so long ago, Kelder accompanied me on a driving tour of the area where he lived and worked when he wrote *The Eye of Revelation* in the late 1930s, North Hollywood and the Hollywood Hills in Southern California. No, Kelder was not a movie screenplay writer, but he did work for a time as a researcher at one of the major Hollywood studios. Surprisingly, many of the landmarks he remembers from those days are still intact, including the house where he lived, perched high atop the Hollywood Hills overlooking Los Angeles and the Pacific Ocean, a stone's throw from the home of movie legend Errol Flynn. Today the modest structure is surrounded by the homes of movieland's rich and famous.

Kelder asserts that Colonel Bradford was a very real individual whom he did encounter in the greater Los Angeles area at that period of his life, though "Bradford" was a pseudonym. Little more than that is forthcoming.

But just as intriguing as Kelder or Bradford is another man whom few know anything about. He is Harry J. Gardener, the man who published *The Eye of Revelation* in 1939 under the imprint of the small publishing company he operated, The Midday Press. Apparently, it was Gardener who first met Bradford, introduced him to Kelder, and asked Kelder to write a book about Bradford's Tibetan adventures.

Kelder is sketchy, at best, when it comes to details on the relationship among the three. Suffice it to say that he and Gardener became lifelong friends who maintained contact with one another until Gardener's death in the 1970s. Bradford, on the other hand, came into their lives and then departed, never to be seen again, much as he did in Kelder's written chronicle.

I suspect, though it is purely conjecture on my part, that though Peter Kelder wrote *The Eye of Revelation* in the first person, he was not the man who befriended the Colonel before his expedition to Tibet and who learned first-hand about the Five Rites upon the Colonel's return. That distinction, I suspect, belongs to Harry Gardener who probably asked Kelder, a capable writer, to draft the story for him, Gardener remaining nameless and Kelder assuming his role. Today, almost 60 years after the fact, it's impossible for even Kelder himself to say just how much of the information in the book was gained through direct contact with Colonel Bradford and how much was gained second-hand from Harry Gardener. It's equally unclear what embellishments, if any, Kelder added to the story.

These lingering issues will never be fully resolved. But does that really matter? As Kelder asserts, they are nothing more than intriguing loose threads which do not weaken the integrity of the garment as a whole. The important questions are, Does his book give something of value to its readers; Does it make a worthwhile contribution to their lives?

I hope the following chapters will help you discover that it does. You must supply the final answer.

Harry R. Lynn
Publisher

CHAPTER ONE

Searching for the Fountain of Youth

by Harry R. Lynn

The story could have been concocted in the head of an overly imaginative Hollywood screen writer. It is that preposterous. At the same time, it is engaging, appealing, and it speaks words of wisdom that seem to resonate with something deep inside.

More than two million people around the world have experienced this curious mix of reactions upon reading *Ancient Secret of the Fountain of Youth, Book 1,* the short volume which precedes the one you are reading now.

As its title suggests, the book's message is one of compelling concern to just about everyone over the age of 40. It tells how to arrest and reverse the aging process, how to achieve the health and vitality of unending youth.

The synopsis that follows is offered for those who have not read Kelder's book. It, together with the chapters that follow, will give you all of the pertinent information contained in *Book 1* and much more. Therefore, it is not essential for you to read it, but it is highly recommended that you do so. In Kelder's book you'll find inspiration and magic that can't be duplicated here. Many people who read the book cherish the experience and return to reread it again and again. It's something you shouldn't miss.

The book's story begins one afternoon when author Peter Kelder is relaxing on a park bench, going through the afternoon paper. Before long, an elderly gentleman seats himself next to Kelder and engages him in conversation.

The old man introduces himself as Colonel Bradford, a retired British Army officer who also served in the diplomatic corps for the Crown. His career has taken him to the far corners of the globe, and Colonel Bradford regales Kelder with tales of his adventures.

When the two part, they agree to meet again. Before long, they are seeing one another regularly, and a close friendship develops.

One evening when they are together the Colonel announces a startling decision he has made. When he was stationed in India some years previously he had heard a curious and unforgettable story. It concerned the lamas of a particular monastery somewhere in the remote wilderness of the Tibetan Himalayas. In that monastery, ancient wisdom handed down for thousands of years promised a solution to one of the world's great mysteries. According to legend, the lamas of the monastery were heirs to nothing less than the secret of the fountain of youth.

Like so many other men, Colonel Bradford had become old at the age of 40, and since then he had not been growing any younger. The more he heard of this miraculous fountain of youth, the more he became convinced that such a place actually existed. He began to gather information on directions, the character of the country, the climate, and other data that might help him locate the spot. And once his investigation had begun, the Colonel became increasingly obsessed with a desire to find this fountain of youth.

The desire, he told me, had become so irresistible, he had decided to return to India and search in earnest for this retreat and its secret of lasting youth. And Colonel Bradford asked me if I would join with him in the effort.

Should he go with Colonel Bradford? Kelder agonizes over the decision, but finally sides with skepticism, reluctantly declining to go.

Yet in the back of my mind the haunting possibility remained: a fountain of youth. What a thrilling idea! For his sake, I hoped that the Colonel might find it.

Colonel Bradford sets out on his mission alone. Then, years pass without word from him. In fact Kelder has nearly forgotten his erstwhile companion and notions of a Tibetan Shangri-La when one day a letter arrives announcing that the Colonel has achieved his goal and will shortly return.

Soon thereafter, when the two are reunited, Kelder is witness to an astonishing transformation. Amazingly, Bradford looks, "as the Colonel might have looked years ago in the prime of his life. Instead of a stooping, sallow old man with a cane, I saw a tall, straight figure. His face was robust, and he had a thick growth of dark hair with scarcely a trace of gray."

Colonel Bradford proceeds to tell his very excited friend all that has happened during his extended absence. He tells of years of struggle and effort finally rewarded with success—the discovery of a remote Tibetan monastery whose occupants never grow old.

In the monastery, older men and women were nowhere to be seen. The lamas good-naturedly referred to the Colonel as "The Ancient One," for it had been a very long time since they had seen anyone who looked as old as he. To them, he was a most novel sight.

"For the first two weeks after I arrived," said the Colonel, "I was like a fish out of water. I marveled at everything I saw, and at times could hardly believe what was before my eyes. Soon, my health began to improve. I was able to sleep soundly at night, and every morning I awoke feeling more and more refreshed and energetic. Before long, I found that I needed my cane only when hiking in the mountains."

Then, one morning the Colonel stumbles onto a mirror, and for the first time in two years he sees his reflection. To his utter disbelief and amazement, the image before his eyes is that of a much younger man. The Colonel realizes that he has undergone a physical transformation: he appears to be at least 15 years younger than he was the day he arrived.

"Words cannot describe the joy and elation which I felt. In the weeks and months ahead, my appearance continued to improve, and the change became increasingly apparent to all who knew me. Before long, my honorary title, 'The Ancient One,' was heard no more."

Then, Colonel Bradford proceeds to explain exactly how he achieved this remarkable feat of rejuvenation.

"The first important thing I was taught after entering the monastery," said the Colonel, "was this:

the body has seven energy centers which in English could be called vortexes. The Hindus call them chakras. They are powerful electrical fields, invisible to the eye, but quite real nonetheless. These seven vortexes govern the seven ductless glands in the body's endocrine system, and the endocrine glands, in turn, regulate all of the body's functions, including the process of aging...

"In a healthy body, each of these vortexes revolves at great speed, permitting vital life energy, also called prana or etheric energy, to flow upward through the endocrine system. But if one or more of these vortexes begins to slow down, the flow of vital life energy is inhibited or blocked, and—well, that's just another name for aging and ill health.

"...The quickest way to regain youth, health, and vitality is to start these energy centers spinning normally again. There are five simple exercises that will accomplish this. Any one of them alone is helpful, but all five are required to get best results. These five exercises are not really exercises at all. The lamas call them rites, and so that is how I shall refer to them, too."

That said, the Colonel describes and demonstrates for Kelder five yogic exercises which he calls "the Five Rites." He tells Kelder to begin performing each rite three times daily, then to gradually increase repetitions until he is performing each rite 21 times a day.

Later, he explains that benefits from the rites will be more pronounced for those who practice celibacy. While he cautions that celibacy is not a realistic goal for most people, he offers a sixth rite which will be helpful to those who are up to the challenge.

In Chapter Five of this book, all six rites are described and discussed in detail. The chapter also offers advice which will be helpful to those who experience difficulty performing any of the rites, and guidelines which will help everyone perform the exercises effectively and safely.

Once Bradford has revealed the Five Rites, Kelder enthusiastically begins to experiment with them. Within three months he experiences impressive results. He is eager to share the news of Colonel Bradford's discovery with others and asks the Colonel if he will lead a class. The Colonel agrees, and the small study group which results is dubbed "the Himalaya Club." The group meets regularly to practice the Five Rites and discuss related matters such as diet and nutrition (see Chapters One and Six). Sure enough, the members of the club—all over the age of 50—are within short order benefiting from the Five Rites' rejuvenative powers.

Since the modest inauguration of Colonel Bradford's first Himalaya Club, readers of Kelder's book have carried the torch forward, organizing their own groups and classes and often borrowing the name Himalaya Club. In this manner countless people in nations around the world have participated in Bradford's fountain of youth discovery. For further information about starting your own Himalaya Club, see Appendix A at the end of the book.

In the final pages of Kelder's book, Colonel Bradford speaks to gatherings of the original Himalaya Club on two subjects related to health and the Five Rites:

- The first subject is diet. Bradford argues for the importance of limiting the number and the combination of foods eaten at each meal.

- The second subject is voice. The Colonel discusses the

energetics of the human voice, and their relationship to the Five Rites.

In this book, Chapter Six, "Food Combining and Other Dietary Advice," and Chapter Seven, "Energetics of the Voice, Sound, and Meditation," explore both subjects in detail. Each chapter will give specific advice, and each will be of interest and value to anyone who has found Colonel Bradford's summary comments intriguing.

In the end, Colonel Bradford says good-bye to the members of the Himalaya Club as he sets off on a mission to spread news of the Five Rites to others.

"It has been most gratifying to see each of you improve from day to day," concludes the Colonel. "I have taught you all that I can for the present. But as the Five Rites continue to do their work, they will open doors to further learning and progress in the future. In the meantime, there are others who need the information which I have taught you, and it is time for me to be on my way to them."

At this, the Colonel bade us all farewell. This extraordinary man had earned a very special place in our hearts, and so of course we were sorry to see him go. But we were also glad to know that before long others would be sharing the priceless information he had so generously shared with us. We considered ourselves fortunate, indeed. For in all of history, few have been privileged to learn the ancient secret of the fountain of youth.

Peter Kelder tells us that he has used a pseudonym for his book's leading character. But what about the rest of his story?

Should we believe it? Is it fact or fiction? Have other Western travelers to Tibet returned with such remarkable tales?

In the 1920s and '30s, before Kelder's book was written, was it possible to penetrate the wall of secrecy and the physical barriers that isolated "Forbidden Tibet" from the rest of the world, to travel into "the Land of Snows" in search of hidden settlements and arcane mystical secrets? Could it be true that somewhere in the shadow of the world's tallest mountains there existed a Shangri-La where ageless men and women lived in utopian splendor?

We now turn to these questions.

Harry Lynn is the publisher of Harbor Press.

CHAPTER TWO

Westerners Search for the Magic
and Mystery of Tibet

by Richard Leviton

"The most stupendous upheaval to be found on the face of our planet" is how an early 20th century traveler described the mysterious and enigmatic mountain kingdom of Tibet.

Roughly the size of Western Europe, the Tibetan plateau stands three miles above sea level in the heart of Central Asia, surrounded and guarded by the tallest mountains on Earth. Its only doorways are treacherous mountain passes which soar upward to 20,000 feet. Until the Chinese invasions in the 1950s, Tibet was almost completely isolated from the rest of the world, primarily because of this formidable topography.

But like Colonel Bradford, in the early decades of this century a few intrepid travelers did attempt to penetrate the barriers that guarded Tibet and experience first-hand the surprises that lay within. Many failed or died in the attempt. But some succeeded, and when they returned to the outside world they brought with them stories of a land of magic and mystery. They told of supernaturally-empowered lamas, flying mystics, living Methuselahs and death-defying, miracle-performing sages.

Even as late as 1950 Lowell Thomas, Jr., the well-known

Monks at Palkhor Chode Monastery, Gyantse (c. 1930)
Early Western travelers to Tibet discovered an intensely spiritual culture
where fully one-quarter of the male population studied in monastic universities called *gonpas*. Pictured here is one of the methods of instruction,
a form of highly animated debate.

American adventurer, in writing of his recent trip to the "sealed and silent land" of Tibet, said, "The mysterious mountain kingdom beyond the towering Himalayas on the very roof of the world has long been the number one El Dorado for explorers and travelers with a keen appetite for the unknown."

Those travelers who surmounted the physical obstacles to gain entry into Tibet found themselves in an intensely spiritual culture. Before the invading Chinese destroyed its monastic system, Tibet had more than 6,000 Buddhist monasteries, well over 600,000 monks, and 4,000 lamas. Fully one-quarter of the male population studied in spiritual universities called *gonpas* that housed massive libraries containing ancient and irreplaceable handwritten manuscripts.

Travelers to Tibet also found themselves in a closed society that did not welcome outsiders. As Peter Hopkirk writes in *Trespassers on the Roof of the World*, beginning in the 1860s "a succession of trespassers—including mystics, plant-hunters, explorers, and pure adventurers—now began to cross illegally into Tibet." Some sought to plunder the assumed riches of a land whose capital, Lhasa, was called "The Forbidden City." Others wished to advance their reputations as adventurers.

In these goals, few succeeded. But others who genuinely sought spiritual illumination fared better. One of the first such travelers to enter Tibet was Evariste Huc, a Roman Catholic missionary from France who in 1846 reported on his experiences in the monastery of Kounboum. Europeans read with astonishment his accounts of miraculous happenings, such as lamas effortlessly traveling great distances in bodies seemingly made of mist and dream.

Living Among the Great Ones

Rumors of such magic drew a Russian woman named Helena P. Blavatsky (1831-1891) into Tibet beginning around 1857. She would spend, on and off, seven years there living and studying with high spiritual masters. She called them *Mahatmas* (Great Ones), "the perfect ones or accomplished ones," and saw them as possessing some of the oldest and possibly purest wisdom teachings in the world.

Actual travel details of Blavatsky's journeys are sketchy; her own accounts emphasize the teachings she gathered. However, it's believed that she journeyed on horseback or by yak through Tibet in search of "the highest knowledge and power."

After she returned to Europe, and during the time she lived in America, Blavatsky claimed to be in continuing contact with Tibetan spiritual masters. She said they often appeared before her in her New York City apartment, spoke with her, dictated new passages for her books, and demonstrated esoteric principles. Few who met Blavatsky doubted that she was a clairvoyant of exceptional abilities, and her command of esoteric knowledge persuaded many that her claims of contact with the Himalayan masters must surely be true.

Others who later followed in Blavatsky's footsteps, Colonel Bradford presumably among them, are indebted to her for blazing a trail to the East upon which later generations could travel. As early as the 1860s Blavatsky showed the West that spiritual wonders and extraordinary teachings were to be found in Tibet.

Scientists Witness Tibetan "Miracles"

For the skeptical among us, there is much more documentation of Tibet's spiritual wonders in the writings of Baird T. Spalding (1858-1953), a university-trained scientist who orga-

Helena P. Blavatsky (1831–1891)
Beginning around 1857 Madame Blavatsky journeyed through Tibet in search of "the highest knowledge and power." What she learned at the hands of high Tibetan spiritual masters formed the core of the Theosophical movement, which she founded in the late 19th century.

Photograph of portrait by Herman Schmiechen.
Courtesy of the Theosophical Society in America, Wheaton, Illinois.

nized a research expedition to Tibet beginning in 1894. It included eleven scientifically-minded people, and its goal was to study the great Himalayan masters, their feats, and their wisdom.

The members of the expedition were not disappointed. According to Spalding, he and his fellow travelers witnessed miracles of overcoming death, thought transference and telepathy, levitation, flying through the air, walking through fire, and walking on water. For a group of practical scientists trained to take nothing for granted until it is fully verified, the experience was eye-opening. "We went thoroughly skeptical and came away thoroughly convinced and converted," Spalding wrote. Among Spalding's remarkable discoveries was the existence of men and women who said they were hundreds of years old. Spalding claimed that many of them were over 500 years old, and they had records to prove it. One day he and his company had breakfast with four extraordinary men. One said he was a thousand years old, yet his body was as buoyant and supple as that of a man of 35. The man next to him claimed he was 700 years old, and he had the body of a vigorous 40-year-old. Spalding's guide, a master named Emil, claimed he was 500 years old, and another master called Jast said he was about the same age as Emil. Others in Emil's unusual family included a nephew, age 115, and a niece, 128, both as sprightly as if they were in their thirties. Emil's mother was said to be 700 years old. All of these centenarians were as nimble and light-hearted as though they had been 20, Spalding wrote.

What was their secret? They had learned how to achieve extraordinary longevity by "perfecting" the body. Perfecting the body means so mastering its biochemical elements that you can dissolve it and recreate it as you wish. You can change your body of flesh and bone into a body more like mist and dream and travel in it effortlessly on your spiritual journeys to the higher planes. Physical death ceases to have any meaning or

Baird T. Spalding (1858–1953)
A university-trained scientist, Spalding organized a research expedition to Tibet in 1894. He returned with reports of miraculous feats of longevity, levitation, flying through the air, and walking on water.

Baird T. Spalding, author of Life & Teaching of the Masters of the Far East, *Devorss Publications, Venice, California.*

reality when seen in the light of this accomplishment. Surely this is astounding, yet the Tibetan masters told Spalding that this feat ought not to be regarded as exceptional. Each of us is given a spiritually perfect body that is capable of living many centuries, explained Emil. These people have merely learned how to restore their bodies to that pristine state.

At least something of this Tibetan ability to live for a very long time must have rubbed off on Spalding, for he lived to be 95. According to a close friend, he had almost unlimited energy, was almost never fatigued, and could survive on four hours of sleep a night for weeks on end. He maintained that high vitality up until the end of his long life. Had he perhaps found a fountain of youth?

Tibetan Secrets Are Revealed to the West

Among the first Westerners ever to travel through Tibet was the French Buddhist scholar, Alexandra David-Neel (1868-1969). A pioneer feminist almost a century ahead of her time, she holds the honor of being the first Western woman to set foot in Lhasa (at age 54) and to be officially received by a Dalai Lama.

Because traveling in Tibet was so dangerous, David-Neel and a Tibetan lama companion had to disguise themselves as naljorpas, or beggar-pilgrims. It was only through anonymity and disguise that they could safely move through the country; still they had to fend off roaming bandits and government police. And the British government constantly sought to expel her from Tibet as would Tibetan officials, had they known the truth of her disguise.

In all, David-Neel spent more than twelve years in Tibet from approximately 1912–1924. She recorded her considerable exploits and discoveries in a series of popular books which are still in print and still exciting to read.

Alexandra David-Neel (1868–1969)
At age 54, David-Neel became the first Western woman to set foot in the Tibetan capital of Lhasa, where she was officially received by a Dalai Lama. During her 12-year stay in Tibet she witnessed the mysterious and seemingly magical accomplishments of adepts, masters, sages, and sorcerers.

David-Neel was a practicing Buddhist. She studied Tibetan culture and language under the supervision of the Panchen Lama, who was Abbot of Tashilumpo, a monastic university-city which was the Tibetan equivalent of Oxford or Harvard. Situated near Shigatse, it housed 3,800 monks and had an immense library. There she earned the equivalent of a Ph.D. in Buddhist studies and was awarded honorary lama's robes. For any Westerner, much less a French woman, to earn this distinction in Tibet was truly extraordinary—and still is. His Holiness, the 14th Dalai Lama, Tenzin Gyatso, says of David-Neel that she was "the first to introduce the real Tibet to the West" and to "convey the authentic flavor of Tibet as she found it."

While David-Neel's story is quite compelling, the real value of her considerable efforts is in the teachings she brought back for us. Like Blavatsky and Spalding, David-Neel brought back stories of mystic and spiritual prowess so remarkable that Colonel Bradford's reported experiences pale in comparison. She described the extraordinary abilities of various "psychic sportsmen" she encountered in her travels. In fact, David-Neel herself was an accomplished adept for she was initiated in a number of Tibetan rites, and she occasionally demonstrated her accomplishments.

For example, there is the ability to sit naked on a frigid snow peak wrapped in blankets immersed in freezing water, then to turn the water to steam and thoroughly dry the blanket. This feat is accomplished by mastering a form of breathing called *tumo*. The idea is to generate heat within the body by combining a particular style of breathing with certain thoughts and visualized images. All of this intensifies inner heat within the solar plexus (see Chapter Four). If the practice is performed correctly, one actually starts to feel warm all over.

David-Neel, who had always suffered during cold weather, mastered tumo breathing to a degree that enabled her to go

Tumo breathing, demonstrated by a hermetic yogi. Early Western travelers to Tibet, among them Alexandra David-Neel and W.Y. Evans-Wentz, reported on this remarkable phenomenon. Tumo practitioners could sit naked in the snow, wrapped in blankets immersed in freezing water. They were then able to turn the water to steam and thoroughly dry the blankets.

Photograph by Thomas L. Kelly from Tibet, Reflections from the Wheel of Life, *published by Abbeville Press, New York, 1993.*

about Tibet in relatively light clothing. Tumo made her free from fear of the cold and from the cold itself.

Centuries earlier, one of Tibet's preeminent yogis had championed tumo for its practical value as an alternative to heavy winter clothing. Tumo adepts could comfortably sit in the frozen mountains wearing nothing more than cotton clothing. Monks melted the ice off blankets as a way of demonstrating their mastery of tumo breathing.

David-Neel also witnessed *lung-gom* (trance walking). This is the ability to stride rapidly across the landscape for days on end without stopping for food or water. Masters of lung-gom move as if flying over the ground, which is how many have described this awesome skill of sustained fleet-footedness. The Tibetan lamas master this after difficult training involving breathing exercises, chants, and visualizations. The key to lung-gom is to concentrate the mind on the element of air and on all its associations, especially that of lightness. You do this so intensely that you become, in practical terms, identified with air.

David-Neel describes one *lung-gomp-pa* who had so mastered the skill that he had to wear heavy iron chains just to stay on the ground and to keep from floating off. Watching another trance walker, David-Neel noted that he didn't run, but rather he "seemed to lift himself from the ground, proceeding by leaps." His face was perfectly calm and impassive, his eyes wide-open, fixed on a distant object in space. His steps were as regular as a pendulum and he moved with the elasticity of a ball, rebounding each time his feet touched the ground. "My servants dismounted and bowed their heads to the ground as the lama passed before us, but he went his way apparently unaware of our presence," she wrote.

Trance walkers, while maintaining this state, could cover tremendous distances in a short time and arrive without appearing to be at all tired. Clearly this was a feat of practical value in this sparsely populated land of difficult terrain.

Evans-Wentz's Work Lends Credibility to Bradford's Claims

If the practice of lung-gom trance walking were taught universally in Western schools, it would eliminate the need for all forms of motorized transport, even bridges, observed W.Y. Evans-Wentz, an American scholar who sojourned in Tibet between 1917 and 1922. Furthermore, he said, tumo breathing would eliminate the need for central heating.

Based on what he had learned in Tibet, Evans-Wentz believed that the powers of yoga, both mental and physical, were unsurpassed. "The supreme Magician in yoga is Mind," he explained. "By controlling his mind, a master of yoga can control everything in the physical world, even the atom." Evans-Wentz's words echo those of Colonel Bradford, whose Tibetan fountain of youth included a series of yogic exercises reinforced with mental magic.

Like David-Neel, Evans-Wentz was a pioneer in the introduction of Tibetan teachings in the West. And like her, he not only reported on miracles of spiritual accomplishment, he also explained how to achieve them—something Colonel Bradford would also do when he followed in their footsteps roughly one decade later. It's interesting to note once again that the accounts of those who preceded Bradford tend to validate his far-fetched tale.

Youthfulness and the Power of the Mind

"Strange things, seemingly contrary to all known laws of nature, are reported again and again by the few travelers who have been able to come into close contact with Tibet and its inhabitants," observed German writer Theodore Illion in the 1930s. These reports of miraculous accomplishments and mysterious secrets so fascinated the German-born traveler that he set

The Monastic University at Tashilumpo (1907)
Here Alexandra David-Neel studied under the Panchen Lama. She earned
the equivalent of a Ph.D. in Buddhist studies and was awarded honorary
lama's robes.

© The Hedin Foundation, The National Museum of Ethnography, Sweden.

out on his own for Tibet in the mid–1930s. He wanted to see it firsthand, to meet its fabled cave-dwelling hermits, to personally witness the strange and miraculous phenomena of which he had read.

Like those before him, Illion traveled furtively and in disguise, and his journey exposed him to great difficulty and constant danger. But in the end, Illion's efforts were rewarded. He, like David-Neel, witnessed such marvels as lung-gom trance walkers, the flying lamas who vaulted across the landscape in seeming defiance of the laws of gravity.

Like Baird Spalding, Illion was also keen to meet Tibetan lamas who had mastered the art of physical longevity, the cave-dwelling hermits who managed to remain young almost indefinitely. He had heard rumors that some hermits lived to be 500, even 600 years old.

Illion met and stayed for five days with one such man, a hermit who appeared to be about 30 years old, though his actual age, we are told, was 90. One day during a two-man exercise, Illion clasped the hermit's body. "It was elastic and lithe, like the body of a boy of 19," he discovered. The man told Illion that he hardly ever ate anything and spent most of his time fasting. "Is this then why you look so young," Illion asked him. "No," replied the hermit. "It's being free from the poisons of fear, worry, and anxiety that keeps me young." One of the keys to a supple longevity is the art of relaxation, explained the hermit. This is not the luxury of a soft chair, but the ease of a mind that does not indulge worry, fear, or anxiety, he told Illion. You must find this state of psychic relaxation, of being rather than having. When you always want to gain something, this puts you into a state of being cramped, both mentally and physically. A lifetime of inner cramping ages your mind and body and eventually ends your life.

Theodore Illion, a German-born traveler who journeyed to Tibet in the mid-1930s. Like David-Neel before him, he witnessed such marvels as the flying lamas called lung-gom trance walkers.

Most important, if you want to remain young, you must feel young, the hermit continued. Youthfulness is not something that can be achieved purely by practices. If you are old at heart, if you feel and act old, physical old age will quickly follow, regardless of diets or practices. Nor can you achieve perpetual youth by drinking some elixir of immortality. To achieve youthfulness, first you must make an inner effort of will and have a true change of heart and view. Youth is foremost a quality of mind and freedom from habitual ways of thinking and living.

Again, we find shades of this view in the words of Colonel Bradford. The key to making the Five Rites work, says Bradford, is mental attitude. If you are to become younger, you must mentally erase the concept of aging, and replace it with the image and feelings of youthfulness. Says Colonel Bradford, "If you are able to see yourself as young, in spite of your age, others will see you that way too."

Longevity Secrets from a Contemporary Lama

The published accounts of Tibetan travelers from the late 19th and early 20th centuries make it clear that, whether or not the story of Colonel Bradford's Tibetan expedition was factual, it could easily have been so.

But what of the Five Rites themselves? Are they authentic? Was there a tradition of longevity teachings in the Himalayan region that might put the Five Rites into the context of traditional instruction? After all, Colonel Bradford surely didn't pluck the exercises out of thin mountain air.

This much we know: There are many stories in Buddhism about attaining long life through special practices. They include numerous Tibetan legends about highly accomplished, nearly superhuman adepts called *Mahasiddhas*—men and women who have attained a high degree of spiritual enlightenment and make themselves available to teach students. Among the Mahasiddhas known for attaining immortality or extraordinary longevity, and for remaining on Earth to instruct humanity in this were the *Nath Siddhas*. It is believed that many of the most important Nath Siddhas are still alive and meditating even today in secluded Himalayan caves. They have vowed not to leave the physical plane until all human souls are saved from suffering.

Lest we form the impression that tales of Nath Siddhas and near-immortal lamas are the stuff of ancient folklore, the contemporary example of a well-known Tibetan *rinpoche* (revered teacher) offers another perspective. He is Namkhai Norbu (1938–), who lives in Italy. Norbu is one of the best-known contemporary Tibetan teachers and has authored several books in English.

According to Tibetan belief, great masters of the past hid their wisdom teachings for the future, literally burying them in caves. It is the responsibility of lamas in a later time, such as ours, to find these buried teachings and reveal them to the world.

One day in 1984 while meditating in Nepal in a sacred cave, Namkhai Norbu discovered an authentic longevity teaching. He received it in an unusual manner, through a series of dreams and meditations. It was in this sanctified cave, known as the Cave of Long Life, that two famous Tibetan masters had attained immortality many centuries earlier. Namkhai Norbu appreciated the situation: a secret practice for developing a long and firm life was now being miraculously revealed to him by ancient masters. It was up to him to write it down for the benefit of his many students in the West. The material included chants, special exercises for breathing and energy control, visualizations, and instructions pertaining to chakras and energy channels in the body. Norbu now teaches these longevity practices to his students in the United States and Europe.

Again we have a parallel, this time contemporary, which

lends credibility to Colonel Bradford's story. The matter of chakras, or energy circuits in the body, is central to Colonel Bradford's Five Rites (see Chapter Four). The discovery by a living Tibetan rinpoche of ancient teachings that also relate longevity practices to energy fields in the human body adds further substance to Colonel Bradford's account.

For those who encounter a stumbling block in the outlandishness of the Colonel's story, this chapter should help bridge the believability gap. In it, we have discovered that Tibetan adventurers of the late 19th and early 20th centuries witnessed miraculous and magical happenings and beheld extraordinary feats of longevity. The historical record they have left us supports the substance, if not the details, of Colonel Bradford's reported experiences. In light of these eyewitness accounts, surely it is not unreasonable to believe that perhaps, more than half a century ago, Colonel Bradford did bring us something genuine from the "sealed and silent" mountain kingdom.

Richard Leviton has been a natural health journalist for twenty years. He was Senior Writer for East West Journal (now Natural Health), Yoga Journal, and The Quest, and is the author of numerous books, including The Imagination of Pentecost *(Anthroposophic Press, 1994),* Brain Builders *(Prentice Hall, 1995), and* Looking for Arthur *(Station Hill Press, 1995). Leviton is currently Executive Editor of* Alternative Medicine Digest *and* Future Medicine Publishing.

CHAPTER THREE

True Stories of Healing
and Rejuvenation

by Laura Faye Taxel

It was one of those sultry dog days in late August when the phone rang with a call that, hackneyed though the phrase may be, was to change my life. A voice on the other end of the line introduced the caller as an editor from Harbor Press. She explained that she had seen an article I authored in a national magazine and was interested in working on a book project with me. My writer's heart pounded with excitement at the opportunity.

When she began to explain that the subject involved a companion volume to a book titled *Ancient Secret of the Fountain of Youth*, I was, to say the least, a bit skeptical. My job, she told me, would be to interview people who had successfully been using the Tibetan exercises described in the book, called the Five Rites, to reverse the aging process and achieve good health. It sounded intriguing, but unlikely.

I read *Ancient Secret of the Fountain of Youth* and like many people I later spoke with, my initial reaction was that it all sounded too good to be true. The publisher sent me copies of letters he'd received recounting near miracles — emotional narratives of rejuvenation and cure. People insisted the Five Rites had brought them complete relief from crippling arthritis, full recovery from stroke, and taken 10 to 20 years off their appearance. The very idea that such a simple practice could have such incredible effects seemed far-fetched, and I found it all hard to believe. But I decided to do the rites myself, reasoning from a professional point of view that I couldn't talk with other people about their experiences unless I had some real experiences of my own. In truth, I was also just plain curious. Could these five simple exercises really deliver all they promised?

Six months later, the life-changing quality of that phone call was clear to me. It was not the contract I subsequently signed with Harbor Press that proved so worthwhile, or even the project itself which gave me a chance to talk with so many wonderful, interesting, and inspiring people. The true significance was in the book and the material it contained. Doing the Five Rites brought a new kind of energy and well-being into my days. I found I was handling the stress of my busy life as a wife, mother of three, and full-time writer better than ever before. I could see and feel the changes in myself; I hadn't felt so good or been so healthy in years.

I was so excited by these discoveries that I began to encourage everyone I knew to try the rites for themselves. What began as an assignment for me became an integral part of my life. Eventually, my husband added the rites to his morning routine and so have two of my best friends. At parties, when people ask about my work, I often end up on the floor demonstrating the five postures, sounding more like a saleswoman than an author.

So I can make no claims to being either objective or scientific in my research. I approached each person I interviewed as a fellow-enthusiast, and all were eager to trade "war" stories with me. I'm 43 and I spoke with people twice as old and half my age. The common ground was how the rites had helped us to feel better and live more fully. Talking with others, many with rare or serious health problems, only served to confirm what I had learned for myself. The rites have something of real value to offer those who do them and the elusive fountain of youth is, in fact, very accessible to all. The amazing stories of recovery and rejuvenation that people shared with me dispelled any lingering doubts I may have had about the truth of that. John Cramer is one of the people who shared his story with me.

Pain-Free, Up, and Running:
One Man's Journey Back to Health

John Cramer is 42 years old, a high school English teacher in Long Beach, California.[1] He's married and has two daughters, ages 3½ and 6 months. And he thinks that what he's experienced since starting the Five Rites is tantamount to a miracle.

In his late teens he began to develop severe spinal problems which were later diagnosed as Ankylosing Spondylitis, a rare in flammatory condition of the spine. In severe cases, the vertebrae fuse together from the bottom of the spine upward, ultimately becoming fixed in a forward curve. Ligaments and tendons ossify and turn to bone. It's a painful condition, often misdiagnosed, that progresses gradually over time, and there is no known cure.

In 1979, when he was nearing 30, John was completely incapacitated for a year as a result of this illness. He explored every medical option, assisted by his father, a professor of medicine at Stanford University, but the doctors had little to offer him except pain medication that, in John's words, "would only mask the problem and create new ones." An x-ray taken during this period showed that John's spine looked like it belonged to a man of 50. A physical therapist told John that most people

---

1 To protect the privacy of the people discussed in this chapter, some identifying information has been changed.

with his condition usually just give up and "fuse." But John responded to his disability in a different way.

"I resolved to do whatever it took to get better. I was open to every possibility," he said. That was a dramatic, even a radical, attitude to adopt. He was raised, as he put it, "in the center lane of the medical mainstream." John's father and brother were both doctors and, up until that point in his life, he also ascribed to fairly conventional ideas about health and healing.

"I tried many systems of exercise and therapy including yoga, biofeedback, and Rosen Bodywork, a technique for freeing the body of painful emotions. I began to learn about Chinese medicine and the idea of energy systems and, when I was in my mid-30s and still having some very difficult periods, someone gave me the name of a medical doctor who was an acupuncturist, as well as an herbalist, and I went to see him. All these experiences gave me a different way of looking at myself and my body. I got a grounding in a new view of what it means to heal yourself and be healthy. But I still didn't have all the answers I needed, and I continued to search."

Several years ago, John heard about *Ancient Secret of the Fountain of Youth*, and he bought the book. He began doing the rites during the Thanksgiving holidays, gradually working his way up to the full 21 repetitions for each. "The changes in my body since starting to do the rites every day are nothing short of amazing," said John. "My spine has more suppleness and my posture has improved tremendously. My stamina has increased; I go longer without tiring, and I've begun to notice that other people tire before me during strenuous activity. The rites helped my entire body become stronger and more flexible. My arms are more muscled than ever before and I have much greater strength in my ankles and legs, and in my wrists. I shouldn't do a great deal of lifting, and at one time couldn't, but now, when I need to, I can, and that includes lifting the baby. I can get down on the floor to play with my kids and back up again easily. Before I started doing the rites, that wasn't possible. And I can run again. I don't mean jogging, I mean real running, sprinting just for the pleasure of it or because I need to get somewhere in a hurry. I've been physically unable to do that because of pain and stiffness. It's probably been 20 years since I could run comfortably. When I picked up my daughter at preschool today, we ran down the block together and I was thinking to myself how nice it was to be able to do that with her.

"The rites have done wonders for my breathing, too. Rite Number Four really opens up my chest. I feel a robustness in my lungs that I never felt before."

Most important is the healing effect the rites have had on John's spine, but there have been other benefits, too. "I had been searching for a time-efficient system of exercise," John explained, "and as soon as I began to do the Five Rites, I realized that they offered body-building strength plus energy, but only required a relatively short amount of time to complete. I try to swim often, but even when I don't have time to get to the pool, doing the Five Rites gives me what I need to carry on with a very busy, stressful life. After doing them in the morning, I'm awake and ready for the day, even if I didn't get enough sleep. And it seems to me that when I do sleep, it's deeper and more restful. I have more energy than I've ever had."

In addition to doing the Five Rites, John has begun to meditate and is currently looking into Ayurvedic medicine, an approach to health which originated in India and is currently being championed in this country by the well-known physician and author Deepak Chopra, among many others.

"I went to hear Dr. Chopra speak," said John, "and I brought a copy of *Ancient Secret of the Fountain of Youth* with me to show him. I wanted his opinion about the Five Rites. He told me that he was familiar with the rites and uses them as part of his own program. This only served to confirm my own experience.

"I started doing the Five Rites 15 months ago and have been almost pain-free for the past year. Simply put, the Five Rites work for me."

P A R T   O N E

Readers Report Dramatic Results

Since the last edition of *Ancient Secret of the Fountain of Youth* was published in 1985, Harbor Press has received hundreds of letters from people like John Cramer expressing their excitement and appreciation about what the Five Rites have done for them. Many readers said that brief testimonials in the front of the book had meant a great deal to them, providing motivation and encouragement. So in January, 1994, the publisher sent out questionnaires to approximately 3,000 people, asking them to share their personal experiences with the Five Rites.

People were asked to rate the book on a scale of 1 to 10. Out of a random sampling of 275, eighty-three percent gave it a 9 or 10. Their overwhelmingly positive feelings spilled over into the margins of our form, where they wrote phrases like "it really works," "uplifting and inspiring," and "try it and believe it." Both Wayne Morris of Cumberland, Maryland, and Lois Munson of Casper, Wyoming, felt compelled to rate the book a 15 in order to let us know just how enthusiastic they felt.

As I studied the responses, I learned that people began doing the rites for a wide variety of reasons. For some, the rites represented a last resort after traditional medicine had failed to help them with a chronic health problem. For others, it was part of an ongoing quest for good health. Pure curiosity was the motivation for some respondents, and for others, it was the onset of aging, a sudden illness, an operation, or an accident. Many people tried the rites because they'd seen how much a friend or family member benefited or because a spouse pushed them into it. Whatever the reason, all quickly became "converts" because the results, which began to be apparent after a relatively short time, were undeniable.

Who's Doing the Five Rites?

Respondents to the questionnaire ranged in age from 20 to 95. Forty percent told us they'd been doing the rites for more than two years, and another 33 percent had been practicing for 6 to 23 months. We interpreted the willingness of so many to continue with the practice as an indication that they were getting some genuine results. Why else would they persist? Those who responded represented virtually every profession from doctors, farmers, and teachers to construction workers and traveling salesmen. They hailed from all over the country, from big cities and small towns, and the only thing most of them had in common was their conviction that the Five Rites had enriched the quality of their lives.

It became apparent that the rites work for all kinds of people of all ages, addressing a huge array of physical needs and adaptable to a wide variety of abilities.

"I like the idea," wrote 32-year-old Bond Bolton of Montgomery, Alabama, "of being able to spend 10 to 15 minutes a day to possibly extend my life another 50 years or more." He's making good progress in that direction. Five months of doing the rites have meant he no longer needs to take his ulcer medication.

Thirty-nine-year-old Laurey Nelson had an accident in 1989 that caused a back injury that left her unable to move, let alone walk, for six weeks. She took a great deal of medication for pain, as well as muscle relaxants. When she came upon a copy of *Ancient Secret of the Fountain of Youth* a year and a half later, she was still having serious problems.

"It took me about six months to work my way up to 21 repetitions," she said. "Every day I felt stronger and better than the day before. I give the Tibetan rites credit for keeping my back in shape. My muscles have an elasticity that I thought was gone, never to return. Unless I am very tired, I don't have to think about my movements; they are natural again. The Tibetan rites are an amazing experience, especially if you think there's no hope for your body. I will continue doing them for the rest of my life. I never want to be immobile again."

Among the more elderly respondents was a 90-year-old woman from Carbondale, Illinois, who had only been doing the Five Rites for two weeks when she wrote to us. She was excited about the fact that in that short time, her blood pressure changed from 190/78 to 178/66. She also noticed that she began to have better equilibrium. "You can be sure," she wrote, "that I am going to continue this wonderful system of improving my health."

Douglas Bly, 91, of Spokane, Washington, took up the practice of the Five Rites four years ago and he also changed his diet. He no longer needs any of the medications he was taking for angina, stomach ulcers, and sinus problems. His failing eyesight and prostate problems are, in his words, "all history now."

From Overall Good Health to a Cure for Colds and Flu

Some people, like Douglas Bly, found that the rites produced a remarkable turnaround, sparking a complete cure or dramatic relief from one or more health problems. Others, like me, noticed a more generalized improvement in their health.

Most noticed a marked increase in energy and stamina, improved muscle tone, and great flexibility and coordination. A majority of respondents said they needed less sleep, and when they did sleep, it was deep and restful. Sixty-one percent told us they looked or felt younger. All who responded to our survey told us about some kind of positive change in their lives as a result of doing the Five Rites.

Many of the people we surveyed said they'd had significant relief and/or recovery from a long list of health problems. For example, sinus congestion with its accompanying headache and pain, chronic sinus infections, migraine headaches, allergies, and persistent and recurrent bouts of respiratory infections such as colds and bronchitis all disappeared completely or diminished in intensity for many people with regular practice of the Five Rites.

Those who do the rites consistently say they have developed better resistance to common ailments like colds and flu. Alice Eggleston, a 65-year-old housewife from Passaic, New Jersey, is just one example. Alice had been vulnerable all her life to sore throats, laryngitis, congested sinuses, and colds. It seemed she had no resistance to any "bug" in the neighborhood. That is, until she discovered *Ancient Secret of the Fountain of Youth* and the Five Rites. "I saw an ad for the book and the whole thing sounded so preposterous, I just had to take a look at it for myself. I read the book and I still thought it was all unbelievable but my natural curiosity prompted me to give the rites a try. I've always had an interest in health, especially natural healing methods, because I've spent so much time being sick ever since I was a little kid. I used to get out of having to do recitations in school because I'd lose my voice so often."

Since Alice started doing the rites two years ago, she hasn't been sick, not even once, and as far as she's concerned that's absolutely incredible. When her husband and son had intestinal flu, she didn't come down with it. And what's more, when she senses that a "bug" may have entered her system, she can get rid of it before it escalates. "The moment I notice those feelings that warn me I might get sick," says Alice, "a little dry scratchiness in the throat or a slight blockage in my nose, I do just the first rite, the spinning one, and the third, the bending backwards, immediately, in addition to the regular 21 of all five each morning, and the symptoms simply vanish. It doesn't develop into a full-blown cold the way it used to. In the past, even though I was very conscientious about taking good care of myself, I still caught colds. These exercises are the only thing that ever did anything for that, and they're the only regular exercises I do. Now I can feel something almost 'take hold,' and I've learned that I can turn it around. This is enough to keep me faithful to the rites forever."

A Cure for Whatever Ails You

A significant number of people were pleased to tell us that since doing the rites regularly they had been able to lower the dosage level or even give up medications for asthma, ulcers, and high blood pressure. Karen Klallam of Porterville, California, gives the rites credit for helping her successfully quit smoking. The practice of the rites also appears to aid in stabilizing blood sugar levels for those diagnosed as hypoglycemic or diabetic. This was even more pronounced for people who also followed the dietary advice given in the book. People also found that adopting both the diet and the exercises helped them with digestive disorders and improved kidney, bladder, and bowel function. They seem to help alleviate leg cramps and stiffness, the symptoms of colitis, and to stimulate an underactive thyroid. People are also adamant about the fact that the rites have had a beneficial effect on eyesight, hearing, and memory, sharpening all the senses.

Painful problems of the back, the spine, the neck, and the joints trouble a large number of people and an overwhelming majority of our respondents told us that the practice of the Five Rites brought immediate and spectacular relief. Among those who regularly visited a chiropractor for these problems, doing the rites has meant that either they no longer needed to go at all or have been able to decrease the number of visits significantly. For those who had been enduring this type of debilitating pain, it was thrilling to be physically comfortable and free to move again.

Arthritis of all kinds is often mentioned as responding extraordinarily well to "treatment" with the rites. Phyllis Specter, 62, of Springfield, Ohio, told us that before doing the rites, she had to creep up the steps one at a time like a little child just learning to walk because of rheumatoid arthritis. "Since I started the rites, I can climb them like I should," says Phyllis.

Women have found some very specific benefits. Sonya Mondale, who went into menopause when she was only 47, found that although she hadn't had a monthly period for a year, after doing the rites for three months, her menstrual periods resumed. Sonya is convinced that "there is a definite rejuvenation going on."

Barbara Kauffman was pleased when after three months of practicing the rites, the symptoms of PMS (premenstrual syndrome), which had affected her lifestyle tremendously, almost completely disappeared. "For at least two weeks prior to the actual start of my period, I was bloated, depressed, and had severe cramps," explained Barbara. "Since doing the rites I only feel some of these things the day before my period starts or on the day it begins. This is a huge benefit."

Forty-four-year-old Mary Shelley's problems with fibroids just disappeared after practicing the Five Rites. She began doing the rites twice a day after being told by her gynecologist that she had fibroids in her uterus. Four months later, a sonogram showed no sign of any fibroids remaining.

Different Problems: One Simple Solution

The Five Rites had a remarkable impact on 44-year-old John Price. "My mother sent me *Ancient Secret of the Fountain of Youth* for Christmas. At the time it arrived I was suffering from extreme lower back pain. I couldn't stand up straight and could barely walk," explained John. He had been kicked by a horse and the ligaments and cartilage in his left knee had been badly damaged. "I couldn't bend my knee and was unable to run," he said. The severe cold of a Maine winter made it even worse.

"I read this book with great excitement," continued John. "I don't take pain medication, so with great difficulty and much pain I started the exercises. From the first round I knew they were extraordinary. This was the only relief from the discomfort of my back and knee that I had experienced in months. I enjoyed the Five Rites and they made me feel great. I persisted in doing them, and after the first week I realized my lower back pain was disappearing. Today, 13 months later, my knee has recovered to about 95 percent, and lower back pain never bothers me. In a very curious way, the rites have also strengthened my will and my memory. My visual and auditory capacities have increased 100 percent. I'm a believer."

Weighing-In With Results

The rites also help to normalize body weight. For people who wished to gain weight, the Five Rites produced a marked and healthy increase in appetite, resulting in an appropriate weight gain. Conversely, those who needed to lose weight have reported shedding pounds, even though they didn't diet.

"I started doing the rites about five months ago," said Carolyn Tudor, 46, of Denver, Colorado. "I have been wanting to take off about 10 pounds for over two years. No diet or amount of exercise seemed to do any good. After two months of doing the Five Rites every day, the 10 pounds disappeared and I have not regained the weight. I also have much more energy. I used to find myself falling asleep on the couch by 9:00 each evening. Now I'm up until between 11:30 and 1:00 a.m. every night. I'm really enjoying my extended hours."

The combination of weight loss and increased energy was even more pronounced for those who not only did the rites, but also followed the book's dietary advice.

Youthing Instead of Aging

Of course, one of the most alluring promises of the Five Rites is that they can postpone aging and restore a youthful appearance and vigor. Everyone over the age of 35 is attracted to the idea of looking and feeling younger. And there is no doubt that for some people, the rites generated a transformation that included the disappearance of skin spots, blemishes, facial wrinkles, and that hangdog look which comes from loose and flabby jowls. Posture improved. For a large number of people, hair that was gray or white returned, at least in part, to its original color. Thinning hair grew thicker and more lustrous. And for 75-year-old James Mayes, four months of doing the rites meant his hair, which had been coming out by the comb-full, not only stopped falling out but began to grow in where he hadn't had any for years.

Both men and women reported that they regained their figures. Others felt that faithful practice of the rites had enhanced their appearances by giving them a "sparkle in their eyes," a "spring in their step," and a "youthful glow."

Doing the rites also seemed to prompt the realization that the concept of old age may be the most debilitating disease of all. Almost everyone accepts the mistaken notion that lethargy, illness, loss of an attractive appearance, decrepitude, and even pain are an inescapable part of life. But for people who do the Five Rites, people who've decided to make every effort to be healthy, it's apparent that there's another side to the story.

Ancient Secret of the Fountain of Youth presents a possibility for the way we live and age that is diametrically opposed to what we're used to. It's natural and easy to dismiss it as unbelievable and to label the five Tibetan rites, which hold out such limitless and optimistic prospects for an alternative, a myth for the wishful or a hoax on the gullible. "The rites are almost like a fairy tale," said Charles Goodwin of Salinas, California. "You wonder how they can work, but they are like magic."

A Boost To Emotional and Mental Health

A shift in mental attitude accompanies physical changes for most people who practice the Five Rites. Most people report having a calmer, clearer, more relaxed state of mind. People as different as a 32-year-old Utah mother of six and an 85-year-old Florida retiree said that doing the rites made them feel good emotionally, as well as physically. Many people had the impression that doing the rites generated a brighter outlook, a more stable temperament, and the ability to think more clearly. "Mentally, I find myself performing at levels I never thought possible," says Lee Woodall, 53, of San Francisco. "[It's] as if the mind of some brilliant, talented person has entered my body. If three short months can produce these results, I am optimistic about the future."

By far, the most consistent comment we received from respondents of all ages was that the practice of the Five Rites gave them a potent sense of well-being, a feeling of happiness with themselves, their lives, and their health. Respondents described the feeling as "a zest for life," "peppiness," "zip," "balance," and "joy." One man called the rites an "effective tonic" and another said it made him "feel like a new man." What became clear was that when people felt better, physically and emotionally, a sense of youthful vitality was not far behind.

"The book gives you hope," says Sara Lurie, a surgical nurse, "and then faith once you start to feel the results from the five Tibetan rites. I started to do the rites in the spring of 1991. Today I am enjoying the fruits of the exercises: much improved health and energy to appreciate my life and help others. My goal was to feel like a teenager again, and it came true."

Out of the hundreds of responses like Sara's that we received, we found those from health care professionals especially interesting. In Part Two of this chapter, you will read about some of these people and learn their remarkable stories. What they have to say will offer more inspiration and hope about recovery, good health, and the possibility of regaining a vitality and joy in living that usually belongs only to the young.

(Turn to Appendix B if you're interested in reading more about personal experiences with the Five Rites.)

PART TWO

A Medical Perspective

The claims made in *Ancient Secret of the Fountain of Youth, Book 1*, can provoke wonder and skepticism. Illness, physical limitations, and deterioration seem like the inevitable outcomes of the passage of time. Modern medicine offers no model comparable to the Tibetan concept of spinning vortexes, and has given only grudging acknowledgment to the relationship between mental attitude, emotional stability, and physical condition. But some members of the medical establishment and other health professionals are beginning to look at ancient beliefs and alternative health care practices with new eyes.

Among the most exciting and encouraging testimonials about the Five Rites are those from people in the health care professions. Not only do they practice the rites themselves, but they also recommend them to their patients. Both their personal and professional experiences have convinced them that the rites can play a significant role in improving overall health.

Robert Cope, M.D., has been exploring alternatives to Western medical practice for more than 20 years and he's convinced that the rites come from an older, broader-based wisdom than our own. "Western medicine treats the body like a car, nothing more than a machine with replaceable parts, and continues to look for single, physical agents as the cause of all our ailments. These exercises contribute to health on more than the physical level.

"I believe there's a connection between emotional pain and physical pain, that health problems are multidimensional and can be related to feelings of anger, bitterness, or negativity," explains Dr. Cope. "The rites work on both levels. They're part of a spiritual tradition, too. Perhaps that's why they don't get boring, as so many other exercise routines do. I can feel that the rites touch me in more than just a physical way."

Dr. Cope, 51, started doing the rites in 1993, as a sort of New Year's resolution. He's now so convinced of their value, based on his own experiences, that he never skips a day. "My muscular strength has improved, my shoulders are straighter, and my abdominal muscles are firmer. After six months, the gray hair at the back of my head began to turn back to its original dark brown. I've gotten my son, who is in medical school, to start doing them, too," says Dr. Cope.

Originally an ear, nose, and throat specialist, Dr. Cope has gradually moved away from the practice of mainstream medicine because he was uncomfortable with the number of surgeries he was performing and the large amounts of drugs he was prescribing, drugs he himself would not want to use. The methods he employs now are outside the boundaries of the traditional training he received in medical school in his native Holland. Working with patients in Scottsdale, Arizona, Dr. Cope uses a variety of techniques to link mind and body in a healing process that addresses both the physical and emotional aspects of illness.

"The Five Rites are not simply exercises for the body. After performing the rites, I have a profound, overall feeling of well-being, a feeling I miss when I don't do them," says Dr. Cope. "I believe they were created to help establish a balance between mind and body." And that's precisely why he's introduced the rites to many of his patients.

Ancient Truth and Modern Science

Health care professionals I spoke with agree that the rites appear to come from a very old and viable healing tradition. "It's my opinion," says Dr. Charles Bowen, a chiropractic neurologist in Billings, Montana, "that the rites were developed over thousands of years as the result of an intuitive understanding of the body and how it works, coupled with careful and concrete observations."

"I bought *Ancient Secret of the Fountain of Youth* several years ago," says Dr. Bowen, "because I liked the idea that it came with a satisfaction, money-back guarantee. I thought that any company making that offer must have a great deal of confidence in its product. And I felt the positive effects of the rites from the very first time I did them. I experienced a dramatic uplift in my awareness both of what was going on inside my body and around me, and a surge of what I'd have to describe as a very stable energy."

Dr. Bowen, one of only 119 board-certified chiropractic neurologists in the world, encourages his patients to do the Five Rites daily. He has a Ph.D. in neurology (the study of the nervous system, which monitors and controls all the functions of the body), and in his very specialized practice he offers options other than surgery and drugs. "Anything that happens in the nervous system," explains Dr. Bowen, "has profound effects on the rest of the body and I have found, both in my own experience and the experiences of my patients, that the Five Rites wake up the entire nervous system. Knowing what I know about how the human body functions, it's not hard to believe the claims of what the Five Rites can do. There is nothing mystical or magical about it."

He uses the book's claim that the rites can help a person look younger to make his point: "Better circulation increases blood flow, especially to the face, bringing fresh oxygen and nutrients to the skin and carrying away waste products. Of course, daily practice of the rites, which stimulates the nervous system, which in turn, controls the circulatory system, contributes to a younger, better-looking appearance."

Dr. Bowen, in practice for more than 15 years, has formulated a very precise explanation of how and why the Five Rites are so beneficial: "The sum total of the body's neurological input and output at any given moment is called the central integrative state. Think of it as a checking account. 'Deposits' come from the mechano-receptors, the specialized sensory nerves of the joints. The highest density of these mechano-receptors are in the region of the head and upper neck, and almost all the rites involve some type of neck flexion or extension.

"These nerves provide a steady flow of sensory information to the brain. Joint movement stimulates the mechano-receptors which increases activity in the cerebellum and the thalamus. These parts of the brain integrate all the information coming in and regulate the sympathetic and the parasympathetic nervous systems that control the involuntary, automatic actions of the body, such as the functions of the heart, lungs, intestines, and glands. The more 'deposits' you make, the better your 'balance' and the more options you have. Lack of stimulation, for example when a person is ill and confined to bed for a long period of time, results in a decrease in the 'account balance.'"

According to Dr. Bowen, one of the primary contributors to premature aging and chronic illness is our sedentary way of life. Lack of movement brings on a sensory slowdown that impacts every system in the body. When sensory nerves don't receive any signals, they begin to atrophy, and that leads to a breakdown in other functions. "The rites work by stimulating the mechano-receptors and raising the central integrative state, which in turn, impacts the immune system, digestion, respiration, cardio-vascular activity, and elimination. This is why practice of the rites can make it less likely that you'll catch cold or flu, delay the onset of degenerative diseases associated with old age, and have a beneficial effect on so many different ailments, from arthritis to sinus problems. I have seen patients with bone spurs, a kind of osteoarthritis that results in a fusion of the affected joints. When the nerves of those joints are stimulated as they are with the rites, the spurs actually dissolve. X-rays have proven conclusively that the spurs disappeared completely, and I believe this came about through a combination of the treatments I provided and the practice of these exercises."

Dr. Bowen, who is 40, has been including the Five Rites as part of his own daily routine for more than five years and says they've replaced his morning cup of coffee because they're a much more effective way to get him going. "When I do the rites, I'm increasing my ability to do all I want to do, maximizing my potential as a human being," says Bowen.

Like Dr. Bowen, Dr. Russell Lewis, who has studied Eastern healing traditions for many years, feels that the Five Rites represent a precise understanding of the human body and how it functions, knowledge that has indeed proven itself over time. He believes the exercises are well thought out, with a kind of credibility that comes from the many experiences of those who have used them. Lewis, a chiropractor in Charleston, South Carolina for over 17 years, cites acupuncture as a similar example of a healing modality that works, and has done so for hundreds of years, despite the lack of a precise scientific explanation.

"In my own three years of practicing the Five Rites," says Dr. Lewis, "I have found that they make me feel wonderful, generating a sense of well-being and harmony. I think this positive effect is the result of the action of ancient Eastern physical and metaphysical principles. These principles are proving to be consistent with the most recent scientific information about the mind-body relationship.

"Long before a patient gave me a copy of *Ancient Secret of the Fountain of Youth*, I was convinced that the mind must participate in real and long-lasting changes in a person's physical condition. Each person must actively play a role in their own health care and assume a level of responsibility... What's important to me about the book is the message contained in the story about what people of any age can do to maintain their own health. I am not interested in living to 120. What's important to me is quality of life, and I think the rites have a great deal to offer. That's why I do them, and that's why I suggest them to some of my patients, which include people of all ages who suffer from a wide variety of infirmities, illnesses, and musculoskeletal problems. I find the rites to be a perfect mind-body discipline."

Dr. Russell Joilette's own story is a case in point. A medical doctor from Hartford, Kentucky, Dr. Joilette retired in 1993, the same year he began to practice the Five Rites. Seven months later he ran into an out-of-town colleague whom he had not seen in a long time. "You can't retire now. You're only about 47, aren't you?" said this friend. Dr. Joilette told him he was in fact 63, but he had to take out his driver's license to prove it.

Before doing the rites, Dr. Joilette was stooped over and unable to turn his head due to an old neck injury. His hair had turned gray-white. He was overweight and felt old. "I have followed the advice in *Ancient Secret of the Fountain of Youth* carefully since June 19, 1993," says Dr. Joilette. " I have lost 20 pounds, have more energy and feel more alert. My hair is brown-black with only a few streaks of gray at the temples and is thicker. I have a full range of movement in my neck, without pain, and stand erect. I walk with a light, springy gait. My sexual desires and my abilities have all returned to normal. All of this is absolutely true. People who have not seen me for four years are astounded that I 'got younger.'"

How the Five Rites Work

Each of the doctors I spoke with explained how and why the rites "work" from the perspective of their own area of expertise. But they shared the view that the rites represent a system of exercise that can have a positive impact on the whole body as well as on the mind if practiced consistently. They were unanimous in finding that the rites improve muscular strength, flexibility, circulation, and respiratory function, as well as enhancing coordination, equilibrium, energy, and mental acuity.

Some doctors feel that the improved circulation produced by the rites aids the body in washing away toxins, wastes, and impurities that are stored in fatty tissue, organs, and joints. Others focus on the fact that the rites generate a better flow of oxygen to the brain which improves its ability to function. Many are convinced that the stimulation of the chakras, or energy centers, described in *Ancient Secret of the Fountain of Youth*, is in fact a stimulation of the endocrine system. (See Chapter Four for a discussion of the chakras.)

"The location of the chakras along the spinal column corresponds to the major endocrine glands," explains Dr. David Selman. "These glands help maintain the homeostatic balance of the body's chemistry and its automatic functions. The thyroid and pituitary glands, which are linked with the production of the growth hormone long associated with aging, are part of the endocrine system. Both are located in the head and neck region, and the rites are especially good for engaging that area and activating those glands. In scientific studies, the introduction of small amounts of this growth hormone have been shown to slow down the aging process."

Dr. Selman, a microbiologist with a special interest in the relationship between the mind, the body, and the immune system, is currently seeking funding for a scientific study of the effect of the Five Rites on the body's ability to manufacture this growth hormone. He brought that same scientific spirit of inquiry to *Ancient Secret of the Fountain of Youth* when he was first introduced to the book four years ago. He wanted to do the Five Rites to see what would happen.

Much to his surprise, Dr. Selman, 63, soon found himself feeling younger and getting healthier. He noticed an increased resistance to common colds and flu. After a month of doing the Five Rites, he was able to play three sets of tennis in the midday heat, something quite impossible for him before. His current partner for doubles is 43, but Selman says he has no trouble keeping up. "I feel better than I did when I was 28. I look better, too. I'm six feet tall, and since including the rites as part of my daily regimen, no matter how much I eat, my weight has stabilized at 133 pounds," says Dr. Selman proudly.

Because he is a scientist, Dr. Selman is reluctant to claim that the rites alone are responsible for his remarkable good health. One person, he explained, cannot constitute a scientifically sound, controlled study. "I can't say for certain how I would feel if I did not do the Five Rites," he says. "All I know is that I do them and have a very strong sense that they are helpful. That's why I discuss them in my seminars and classes."

Focusing On Getting Better

"I'm more concerned about results," explains Kathleen Sortini, M.D., "than I am in how or why things work for my patients. I'm open to whatever can help them. When the best that medical science has to offer isn't effective, I'm all for trying something else. People want to get better, and I share that focus." This attitude made her receptive to the fact that one of her patients, Cynthia, credited the Five Rites with totally transforming her life and her health.

Dr. Sortini, currently a full-time faculty member at the University of South Florida's School of Medicine and Ob-Gyn Coordinator for the Halifax Medical Center Family Practice Residency Program in Daytona Beach, first met Cynthia eight and a half years ago. Cynthia, 27 at the time, had multiple problems including a chronic underactive thyroid, an eating disorder that kept her dangerously underweight, and lethargy so intense that even climbing a flight of ordinary stairs was utterly exhausting. Dr. Sortini took Cynthia on as a patient and also recommended that she begin counseling with a clinical psychologist with whom the doctor worked.

But neither counseling nor medication seemed to help. In Cynthia's own words, she felt "older than most old people," and thought she "was dying." She "felt cold all the time and looked terrible — painfully thin with dull, brittle hair and drooping eyelids." She was barely able to manage the care of her 6-year-old daughter.

Just before becoming pregnant with her second child, Cynthia literally stumbled upon a copy of *Ancient Secret of the Fountain of Youth*. One rainy day, she saw a pile of books stacked on the sidewalk for the trash collector. Sorting through the wet stack to see if anything good was salvageable, she found Kelder's book, the only one that was dry. Intrigued by the title, she took it home, read it, and began to do the rites almost immediately. Both she and Dr. Sortini soon began to notice positive changes in her health. She developed an appetite and began to eat and gain weight. Her energy level and mood improved dramatically. Cynthia was convinced that the rites were responsible.

"I had never heard of *Ancient Secret of The Fountain of Youth* and the Five Rites until Cynthia brought them to my attention," explains the doctor, "and I was skeptical as any doctor would be. But I didn't think the exercises could hurt her in any way, so I wasn't opposed to her doing them. As time went by, I could hardly believe the changes I saw. She was a different person. She looked better, felt better, and seemed to be getting her act together, effectively taking charge of her life and her health."

"When I was pregnant the first time," said Cynthia, "I had to spend the last two months on complete bed rest. Both Dr. Sortini and I were very worried that, being pregnant again, I wasn't going to make it, and if I did, I wouldn't have the energy to take care of the new baby. I even considered putting it up for adoption." But Cynthia's pregnancy proceeded without complication, and she gave birth to a healthy baby five months ago. She did Rites One, Three, and Four up until the day she went into the hospital and was able to do all the rites six weeks after delivery.

"My girlfriend, who had her baby right after me, still looks pregnant. But nine weeks after my daughter was born, you couldn't even tell I'd been pregnant," Cynthia said enthusiastically. "I was doing all 21 of each rite and I felt great. I had incredible energy, which was such a new experience for me. Now I can take care of both my kids, plus a fish and a rabbit. If there aren't two or three things happening at once, I wonder what to do with myself. Once, carrying the baby plus a few bags of groceries into the house would have almost killed me. But I don't even notice the effort these days. My hair looks beautiful, I don't feel cold, and I take no medications for my thyroid. The rites really performed for me. I was a young person in bad shape, but now I've got my youth and my health back."

Dr. Sortini concurs. "As someone trained in the scientific method I cannot categorically state that the changes and improvements I saw in Cynthia were the result of doing the Five Rites. But I am nonetheless very impressed with what I saw after she began to do them. I'm most interested in what works, and there's no doubt that for Cynthia, the Five Rites did," says Dr. Sortini.

Cynthia believes she found the book at the precise moment when she'd reached a turning point. "I was sick and tired of being sick and tired," she said. "The medicines I was taking weren't doing me any good. I felt that I needed something from within to help me but I didn't know what. The Five Rites answered all my questions."

Aging "In Slow Gear"

At the time he first heard about *Ancient Secret of the Fountain of Youth*, Dr. B. S. Mell, a psychiatrist at a residential treatment facility in Jackson, Louisiana, feared he was heading for heart problems. He was 63, flabby, and overweight. When he had been in private practice, he often worked 60 hours a week, but he was no longer able to work even an eight-hour day comfortably. He felt as if he had suddenly begun to turn into an old man.

"I bought the book because I was curious. I was also unhappy with my physical condition," explained Dr. Mell, "and decided I would give the practice three months, a test to see if it could produce results for me. At the end of the third month, I could see remarkable changes in myself."

Doing the rites noticeably increased Dr. Mell's level of energy. Three years ago, before he had learned about the Five Rites, he required eight hours of sleep each night, and was still tired by mid-afternoon. "I used to have only four or five hours each day when I felt at my peak," he explained, "but now, I never feel tired though I am sleeping much less. I rise at 4:00 a.m. feeling refreshed, work productively all day, and feel alert, without that after-lunchtime sluggishness. Even when I go to bed at night, I am not exhausted."

He also lost 10 pounds, which he has not regained, his waistline trimmed down three inches, and his muscle tone began to return. He liked what he saw in the mirror. The chronic sneezing he'd suffered as a result of hypertrophy (an enlargement) of his nasal tissue stopped, and the shortness of breath he'd begun to notice disappeared completely.

"After seeing what happened for me in three months, I decided to continue," said Dr. Mell. "Now, the rites are a habit and I have only skipped doing them five days in all these years. I know that not only do I feel much healthier, but I actually am. I have not had any major illnesses since I started doing the rites. When I did catch a slight cold, I kept on doing the rites and it was gone in two days. I recently had a full lab work-up as part of my physical, and everything is at normal levels. My doctor could not believe he and I are the same age. He has had bypass surgery and looks 10 years older than I do.

"I doubt that practicing the rites can actually reverse the aging process," says Dr. Mell with a chuckle, "but if one has the willpower to do the exercises, I am convinced that the process can be put in slow gear."

The comments of Dr. Mell, Dr. Sortini, Dr. Cope, and all the other health professionals included in this chapter aren't a sales pitch. They don't come from a "snake oil salesman" pushing the elixir of life or a con artist bent on getting your money. The health care professionals, as well as all the other men and women who volunteered to talk with me, received nothing in exchange. Their only reward for sharing their hard-to-believe, but real-life experiences was in the knowledge that their stories might benefit others.

Finding the Fountain of Youth for Yourself

The subjects you've read about in this chapter are real people leading regular lives just like the rest of us. There's nothing supernatural or mysterious about their stories. What makes these people special is that they didn't just dream about some mythical fountain of youth but discovered that the "waters of life" were actually flowing within them. By making a commitment to doing the rites, they were each able to activate their body's own natural ability to heal and rejuvenate itself.

It's clear from all the responses we received that the Five Rites have the astonishing ability to "answer what ails you." They can change the way you live your life or just make it better, bringing about a cure or helping you live with your problems more comfortably. They might make you look younger than your age or feel like you haven't felt in years, and most important, they can change how you see yourself.

Belief is not a requirement. The five Tibetan rites are not a religious practice. The only requirement for beginning a personal exploration into what the rites have to offer is a willingness to try. Despite all the scientific and medical advances of the twentieth century, the willingness to explore new paths to good health and well-being is irreplaceable. But it's something that many have lost touch with. As a society, we have become dependent on experts and the drugs they prescribe. The explosion in biomedical research has led to a tidal wave of new high-tech, high-cost procedures, which tend to overshadow older and simpler ways of dealing with our bodies. What we've sacrificed in the process is an understanding of how to help ourselves.

So the question that remains for every reader is this: If the five Tibetan rites offer even the remotest possibility of good health, freedom from pain, and the chance to keep or regain the best qualities of being young, why not give them a try? All that's really needed is an open mind and 10 to 20 minutes a day.

The people you have read about in this chapter are as real as your neighbor or best friend. They agreed to talk with us simply because they were enthusiastic about the Five Rites and wanted to share their experiences with others.

All of these people claim that the rites work for them in one way or another. In the next chapter we'll explore some of the possible explanations behind the power of these exercises to heal and slow down the aging process for so many people.

Laura Faye Taxel has been a writer, journalist, and researcher for more than 20 years. Her work has appeared in numerous national and local publications including Ladies Home Journal, Parenting, Natural Health, New Age, The Cleveland Plain Dealer Sunday Magazine, The Akron Beacon Journal Sunday Magazine and Cleveland Parent.

Laura is the author of Cleveland Ethnic Eats (Gray and Company, Inc., 1995), and she is currently working on several book projects on a variety of topics, including health and education.

CHAPTER FOUR

Energy Secrets of the Five Rites

by Richard Leviton

Modern science and medicine tell us that the aging process is not reversible. But Colonel Bradford and hundreds of readers who follow his advice (you read their stories in the preceding chapter) claim that they have achieved the impossible, making themselves years younger physically.

In support of that claim, at least three scientists have demonstrated that, contrary to conventional wisdom, physical aging can be slowed down and, often, reversed.

How Meditation Reverses Aging

In 1978, R. Keith Wallace, a UCLA physiologist, demonstrated the direct effects of meditation on aging. He measured three biological markers: blood pressure, vision, and hearing. All three of these factors improved with continuous practice, and Wallace claimed that in these cases biological age was actually working in reverse. Those who had practiced meditation for less than five years had an average biological age (according to physiological tests) that was functionally five years lower than their chronological age would indicate. But those who had practiced meditation for more than five years tested up to twelve years younger in functional biological age. In other words, regular meditation lowers your functional age, making you in effect younger.

Deepak Chopra, M.D., and his colleague, Jay Glaser, M.D., have also demonstrated that meditation reverses biological aging. Chopra is an endocrinologist who has become a best-selling author and national authority on the relationship between meditation, healing, and aging. He presents a case study in his book *Ageless Body, Timeless Mind* which shows that meditation can decrease biological age.

In 1988, Chopra and Glaser conducted a research project to study the effects on aging of a hormone called DHEA. This is the only hormone presently known to decline with age, beginning at 25 when it reaches its peak. Whenever you have a stress reaction, a portion of your DHEA supply is used up to make various stress-related hormones, such as adrenaline and cortisol. Thus DHEA levels are reliable markers for the body's exposure to stress over time. Studies with mice earlier in the decade had shown that when they were injected with DHEA, their natural aging process was reversed and they regained the youthful vigor typical of young mice. So Chopra and Glaser wanted to see if this happened in humans, too.

In human terms, the mice research told Glaser and Chopra that if a person could resist or alter the effects of stress, their DHEA levels would remain high. If that happened, then the otherwise inevitable aging process that accompanied the decline in DHEA levels might reverse itself. Glaser examined the DHEA levels of 328 meditators and compared the results with 1,462 nonmeditators. In all of the women's groups, DHEA levels were higher among meditators; among the men, they were higher in eight out of eleven groups.

To Glaser and Chopra, this proved that meditation reduces biological aging as measured by DHEA levels. The most pronounced differences showed up in the older subjects, Chopra reports. Meditating men over the age of 45 had twenty-three percent more DHEA, while the women had forty-seven percent more. These levels were independent of diet, exercise, weight, and alcohol consumption. Their DHEA levels were what you'd expect in men and women 5 to 10 years younger.

What mysterious mechanism may make such age reversal possible? Do the Five Rites activate or trigger that mechanism, and if so, how? In this chapter, we'll explore possible answers to these intriguing questions.

The Power of Basic Life Energy

The Five Rites, explains Colonel Bradford, work according to a principle of "life energy." Normally, we think of energy in terms of "fuel," carbohydrates or petroleum, for example. But for Colonel Bradford, energy meant something more subtle: the intangible but potent life force itself, the vital energy that controls life.

Performing the Five Rites, the Colonel tells us, stimulates the circulation of this essential life energy throughout the body. The Hindus call this energy *prana*, a term Bradford introduced to his students. According to Hindu belief prana, or literally the "breath of life," circulates throughout the human being, affecting every facet of life, including your thoughts, feelings and physical well-being. While you cannot see this basic life force, you feel its powerful effects every day.

In 1908, Dr. Walter Kilner, a British doctor and researcher, developed a unique device called the Kilner Screen which made the life force of a human being visible through photographs. Kilner explained that the human life force was organized as an energy field or aura around the body, and the Kilner Screen made photographs of this energy field. It also revealed the presence of energy fields surrounding individual parts of the body, such as the thumb, and other living organisms, such as leaves. Kirlian photography, as it has been known ever since, contributed much toward proving that invisible energy fields surround all biological organisms.

More recently, in the mid-1980s, Richard Gerber, M.D., a Michigan family doctor, combined Eastern ideas about life energy with traditional Western medicine in his classic book, *Vibrational Medicine*. Dr. Gerber believes that basic life energy not only underlies the body and mind, it is organized into complex, interrelated energy systems. These energy systems, which Gerber calls "vibrational systems," provide the food and fuel for all the organs and systems of the body. They provide essential "nutrition" for the body's proper functioning, and they influence all glandular, hormonal, neural, and cellular activities. "Vibrational healing systems hold the key to extending current medical knowledge toward an improved understanding, diagnosis, and treatment of human ailments," explains Gerber.

These ideas on basic life energy give you a glimpse into what might be going on when you practice the Five Rites: it appears that somehow the physical movements and postures of the rites trigger the circulation of more life energy throughout the mind and body, or as holistic medicine calls it, the *mindbody*. In the mindbody, there is no separation between psychological and physiological activities. The mind works through the body and the body works through the mind.

Now let's turn to the next piece of information Colonel Bradford gave us. He said that this life force energy moves through a series of energy centers in the body called *chakras*.

Secret Energy Centers in the Body

Eastern spiritual traditions teach that we all have seven secret energy centers arrayed in a column from the groin to the top of the head. They are secret because under normal conditions we cannot see or detect them. They are called *chakras*, which literally means "spinning wheels" because, according to clairvoyants who claim they can see them, they resemble spinning vortexes or wheels. Their shape and motion are apparently most like a vortex, a common shape we see in water spinning down a drain or a hurricane seen from a satellite.

The chakras are said to work with your physical body through the seven ductless glands of your endocrine system. These glands, which are also arrayed from groin to head, regulate the circulation of vital hormones in the body. According to Eastern teachings, life energy moves through the chakras and is distributed to the body through the endocrine system. As the chakras regulate the circulation of energy through the body, the endocrine glands, in response, regulate the hormonal life of the body.

This is entirely consistent with Colonel Bradford's model of the chakras. According to him, an imbalance or shortage of any hormone secreted by the endocrine system is a result of a problem with one or more of the chakras. An endocrine system that is not functioning properly leads quickly to illness, deterioration, aging, even death. Thus the concept of chakras is central to Colonel Bradford's explanation of how the Five Rites affect one's health and the aging process. As he tells his students, chakras are "powerful electrical fields, invisible to the eye, but quite real nonetheless."

The speed of the chakra spin is crucial to the Five Rites, the Colonel explains. In a healthy person, all seven chakras spin or turn very rapidly, moving life force energy upward through the body from the groin to the head. In addition, in a healthy person, all seven chakras spin at the same rate of speed and work together harmoniously. Here you might think of a revolving water sprinkler at full force, spraying prana in all directions.

If one or more of the chakras is blocked and its natural spin is reduced or even stopped, explains Colonel Bradford, life energy cannot circulate. As a result, illness and aging set in. The aging process itself can be defined in terms of the spinning activity or inactivity of these vortexes. An "abnormal condition" of the chakras — lack of spin, wrong rate, or wrong direction of spin — weakens health and brings on old age. This may be the key: speed up the spin of the chakra and you slow down the aging process. So as far as Bradford tells us, the secret of the Five Rites is in the spin speed and harmony of the chakras.

"The quickest way to regain youth, health, and vitality is to start these energy centers spinning normally again," Colonel Bradford tells us. But what is a normal chakra spin? According to Bradford, it's a speed that is appropriate for a strong and healthy 25-year-old man or woman. To achieve this, the first step is to practice Rite Number One — Whirling — which speeds up the spin of all seven vortexes. Whirling is a kind of warm-up for the fine-tuning of each individual chakra, which is accomplished by practicing the other four rites.

What do you find in the average middle-aged man or woman? You're likely to see disharmony and unequal spin rates in the chakras, Bradford tells us. "The slower ones would be causing parts of the body to deteriorate, while the faster ones would be causing nervousness, anxiety, and exhaustion," he explains. In short, chakras spinning either too quickly or too slowly produce ill health. From this we gather that the Five Rites coordinate, even enhance, the spinning of the seven energy centers of the human body; they help distribute pure life force energy to the endocrine glands and in turn to the body's organs and processes. When this happens, the result is longevity and rejuvenation.

How the Chakras Influence Illness, Healing, and Aging

Eastern teachers call the chakras "lotus flowers." That's because, like flowers, chakras have a varying number of petals and a long stem that attaches to the spine. These petals and the whole lotus flower, in fact, are said to spin or revolve as they receive and distribute basic life energy. The number of petals in each chakra ranges from four in the root chakra to one thousand at the crown.

The link between each of the seven chakras and the specific endocrine glands is a matter of minor controversy. Details vary from one expert to the next, but many believe that the chakras, their locations, and their influence on the endocrine glands are as follows:

Chakra	Location	Gland
1. Root or Base	Base of Spine	Reproductive Glands
2. Sacral	Lower Abdomen	Adrenals
3. Solar Plexus	Upper Abdomen	Pancreas
4. Heart	Chest	Thymus
5. Throat	Throat	Thyroid
6. Brow	Center Forehead	Pituitary
7. Crown	Crown	Pineal

However you wish to correlate the chakras and the endocrine glands, the fact that there is a connection is the key to understanding Colonel Bradford's explanation. It is probably most meaningful to think of the chakras in terms of body regions. If you divide the human form into seven regions, such

The Vortex As the Essence of Life

Throughout the ages, human beings have sought unity, stability, and perfection. The one enduring image that has come to represent this ideal for people all over the world is the circle. A circle has no beginning and no end. It faces all directions equally. Of all geometric shapes, it contains the greatest amount of area within a given perimeter. From ancient times to the present day, the divine, that force which transcends physical matter, has most often been represented by a circle.

A three-dimensional circle is a ball, or sphere. Possessing great stability and structural integrity, the sphere also contains the greatest amount of volume within a given amount of surface area. It is no accident that all stars and planets take the form of a sphere.

Expressing a circle through the fourth dimension, that of time, initially presents a problem since we only experience time moving in one direction. Therefore, imagine two circles side by side. Start at the nine o'clock position on the left circle and trace the upper half of the circle. Where the two circles meet, move onto the second circle and trace the lower half. In this way, you will see that the expression of a circle through time yields a cycle.

If you look around, you will notice that all kinds of activities exhibit a cyclical variation over time. There is the daily cycle of light and dark, the yearly cycle of the seasons. The tides ebb and flow. The moon waxes and wanes. Our bodies follow a daily regular temperature cycle.

Over the past several decades, researchers have discovered cyclical behavior in fields as diverse as animal populations and stock market prices. The important thing to keep in mind when observing up and down fluctuations is that this is the natural course of action through time.

Now let us go one step further, and express a circle through both time and space. Place your finger above your head and begin to trace a circle, simultaneously moving your finger downward. You will notice that this movement is in the shape of a corkscrew or spiral. This shape represents the circle in time and space. A spiral in motion is known as a vortex. Perhaps the most easily recognized representation of a vortex is a tornado. Using the tornado as an example, you can see that the vortex possesses great energy and power.

If you observe the world around you, you will find the vortex everywhere. Through the use of time-lapse photography, it has been shown that when a seed germinates, it does not shoot straight out of the ground, rather it spirals upward. The pattern of seeds in a sunflower or branches on a fir tree will reveal the vortex, frozen in physical matter.

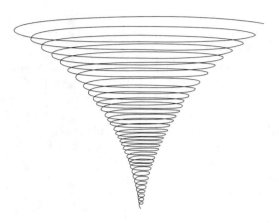

The high and low pressure systems that produce our weather take the shape of a vortex. And this pattern extends throughout the universe. Place a satellite photograph of a hurricane next to a picture of a galaxy, and you will find that they are almost identical.

In the industrial world, the screws and bolts that hold together many buildings and machines are in the shape of spirals.

In our own bodies, spirals are apparent in our fingerprints and in the pattern in which hair grows on our heads. When we breathe, the air circulates in numerous mini-vortices through the nasal passages so that by the time it reaches our lungs it has been warmed, moistened, and filtered, and is now ready for our bodies to use. Perhaps most significant, at the very foundation of our physical selves, the DNA molecules that contain our entire genetic code are in the form of two intertwined spirals.

The vortex is the means by which the powerful energy of the universe penetrates through all levels of existence. Ancient teachings have long instructed that the physical body contains energy centers, spinning vortices through which the energy of the universe enters and vitalizes our bodies. Often as we age, these energy centers become overgrown, as it were, and the flow of energy is impeded. The Five Rites clear away the underbrush so that the powerful, spiraling energy of the universe once more invigorates our bodies.

Charles Albert Marks

as the groin, the stomach, the heart, the throat, the head, and think of each of these regions as under the influence of a single chakra, then you get a simple working idea of how the system might actually be put together.

Since disease is an expression of dysfunction or imbalance in the chakra system, a sore throat is the result of a "sick" throat chakra, and ulcers are the result of a "sick" stomach chakra. This means the energy patterns of the throat chakra or the stomach chakra are somehow out of balance, either spinning too slowly or too quickly.

Clairvoyant Dora Kunz and physician Shafica Karagulla, M.D., claim to have documented over 200 cases linking specific chakras with particular illnesses. In these cases, they say they observed a correlation between the condition of a chakra and a specific disease of the "human system," or the mindbody.

According to Kunz, abnormalities in the chakra petals—color, rhythm, direction of movement, brightness, form, elasticity, and texture—indicate a serious medical condition. Such a condition will probably produce a disease either in the endocrine glands related to that center, or in the part of the body to which the center provides energy. For example, something wrong with the rhythm, color, texture, or energy of the throat chakra may produce a biological problem in the throat. It may be a sore throat, a stutter or speech problem, laryngitis, tonsillitis, or worse.

This corroborates Colonel Bradford's claim that abnormal or unhealthy chakras produce illness and deterioration. It also leads to the probable conclusion that the process works in reverse. In other words, if you correct the balance and spinning of a faulty throat chakra, you improve the health of the thyroid gland and the throat.

Now, if you could find a way to balance all seven chakras and get them working together in the most harmonious way possible, life force energy could flow freely, without restriction, through the seven chakras. The entire endocrine system would benefit, and so would your entire body. Might this in itself slow down the aging process and rejuvenate the body? Could this be the way the Five Rites make this seeming miracle happen?

"Messages" from the Chakras

In addition to affecting your physical health, the seven chakras have a psychological dimension. They send "messages" through your different states of mind, feelings, and perceptions. Even though most of us cannot see the chakras, we can easily tune in to the messages they send us.

Consider these common experiences and the way we describe them: a sinking feeling in my groin; butterflies in my stomach; a pang in my chest; a lump in my throat; a tingling scalp. These are examples of how the energies of the chakras talk to you through different perceptions and states of mind. In moments of sudden fright or panic, such as news of death or serious illness, you may feel a kind of electric shock, almost a vibrating, in the groin. That's because the root chakra, situated here, is being stimulated. This center deals with basic life issues such as physical survival, nourishment, food, money, security, stability, solidity, density, and your biological foundations.

Probably you have experienced the unsettling moment of nervous anticipation known as "butterflies" in the stomach before speaking in public or confronting others, especially authority figures. That's an energy message from the third chakra, the solar plexus center. Its issues are personal expression, self-identity, the exercise of individual will and power. The solar plexus center affects digestion, whether of nutrients, sensory data or ideas.

When you get a lump in your throat, the fifth chakra, or the throat center, is sending a message. The fullness of your feelings (in the heart center) is swelling into the throat, the center of vocal self-expression which relates to communication and self-expression.

While it may be simplistic to summarize the effects of the chakras in this way, it helps us appreciate how their energies affect our lives. Each chakra represents a different fundamental issue. While the first chakra, or root center, pertains to your physical groundedness, the second chakra, located in the vicinity of the genitals, deals with sexuality, reproduction, your emotions, and relationships. The third chakra is about the fire of individual will. The heart center, the fourth chakra, is a mediator among all seven centers; it is the place of compassionate insight, universal love, empathy, the balance between inner and outer concerns, self and world. All aspects of spoken self-expression concern the throat center, the fifth chakra. The brow center, the sixth chakra, located between the eyebrows, facilitates psychic insight, discernment, intuition, the imagination. The center at the top of the head, the seventh chakra or the crown chakra, is the center of pure consciousness, understanding, and spiritual intelligence. Here, if you are receptive, you might receive sparks of divinity—a tingling scalp.

As you can see, the chakras affect every aspect of your life. If, according to Colonel Bradford, you interact with them skillfully by practicing the Five Rites, you will stimulate physical healing and self-development, and reverse the aging process. Your basic life energy will flow freely and abundantly, creating optimal physical and mental health.

Life and Healing in the Sea of Qi

Like the Five Rites, Chinese medicine is based on the power of life force energy, or what the Chinese call *Qi* (pronounced chee). Like prana, Qi is immaterial and invisible, yet it is essential to life. According to Chinese medicine, every aspect of life is affected by the quality and circulation of Qi.

Simply put, if there is no Qi, there is no life. A wilting plant and a feeble person with a weak voice both demonstrate a shortage of Qi. A person with abundant Qi is vigorous and full of energy. For example, children laughing and playing at a party have lots of Qi, but somebody who is sick has greatly depleted Qi; somebody who is irritable has unbalanced Qi. We know through a kind of body intuition what Qi feels like; we know when we have a lot of it or are lacking it. Fortunately, we begin life with a great abundance of Qi. Gaining access to this natural Qi in your own body is at the heart of the Five Rites.

Energy Lines and Acupoints Across the Body

The correct flow and distribution of Qi, like Bradford's life energy, or prana, is essential to good health. Acupuncture, founded on thousands of years of actual clinical use, precisely charts the circulation of Qi through the human mindbody to determine where and how it needs to be adjusted to eliminate disease and illness.

A key concept in acupuncture is that Qi flows through a series of meridians, or subtle energy channels. These meridians traverse the body, from the toes to the head, from the fingertips to the eyes. Along each meridian are numerous points, called acupoints, where Qi may be adjusted—manipulated, increased, decreased, purified—by inserting tiny needles temporarily through the skin.

During an acupuncture treatment, needles are superficially inserted at carefully selected acupoints and left in place for about thirty minutes. While an acupuncturist might object to this image, it is useful in the beginning to think of the acupuncture meridian system as a complex subway and train system traversing the body from head to foot. In this image, think of your body as a great city with dozens of underground rail lines and many hundreds of local stops. Each of these "stops" is called an acupoint; each of the "subway" lines is a route for Qi. In a sense, Qi is the "train of life" coursing through your body, delivering life energy everywhere it goes.

Acupuncturists usually work with fourteen major meridians with several hundred key acupoints on them. But most practitioners agree there are in fact many more meridians and treatment points in the overall system. Traditionally, about 365 acupoints are described, but most acupuncturists are familiar with at least 1,000. All of these acupoints, incidentally, have names and energy qualities that are poetically evocative. Consider these names for Kidney Meridian acupoints: Gushing Spring, Blazing Valley, Great Ravine, Lake of Tears, Shining Sea. Qi circulates constantly through this complex network of energy channels. They are interconnected and linked up with specific organs and physiological systems.

A single meridian relates to a key organ and physiological system of the mindbody. But the meridian relating to a specific organ does not necessarily pass through the organ in question. The Large Intestine Meridian, for example, goes from the tip of the index finger, up the arm to the shoulder, across the neck and cheek, up the nose. It doesn't actually pass through the large intestine. Yet somehow when you stick an acupuncture needle in any of its acupoints, you will be affecting the energy of the large intestine. If you have a large intestine problem, however, you don't necessarily treat the Large Intestine Meridian. You may end up affecting the large intestine by treating several neighboring meridians that influence it. Chinese medicine seems bafflingly indirect. No matter. It all takes place in the sea of Qi, where your mindbody will benefit from the manipulation of energy flow and distribution.

Sometimes practitioners use acupressure massage instead of inserting needles; more often, they use it as a supplement to "needling." When he was studying acupuncture in Beijing in the early 1980s, Harvard-trained physician Dr. David Eisenberg appreciated the wonders of acupressure massage when he received it from an expert named Zhu. Zhu had an uncanny ability to find Eisenberg's "trigger points." These were sites on his body where Qi was temporarily blocked or stagnant. "The pushing and pulling of muscles, tendons, and bones was performed to reestablish or redirect the flow of Qi and recreate bodily harmony," Eisenberg explains. Zhu, by manipulating the points and applying pressure, quickly improved Eisenberg's physical state. This led to a lovely, deeply relaxed condition. Eisenberg described it as "a bizarre sensation of pressure and fullness and heat throughout my body," comparing it to the sense of being keenly aware of every nerve and muscle in his body.

Dr. Eisenberg studied the mysteries of subtle energy firsthand with physicians and martial arts masters in China. In fact, he was the first American medical exchange student to study traditional Chinese medicine in Beijing. We shouldn't be surprised to learn that what he observed completely turned his head around. It did not fit his Western medical model, yet it produced healing and good results nonetheless. People were recovering from illnesses and feeling relief from pain and discomfort simply from the insertion of little needles at certain places in their bodies. Dr. Eisenberg had experienced it himself, despite his skepticism. The results both puzzled and intrigued him, as they do most Westerners schooled in modern science. "I don't know what to believe about Qi," he confessed to a Chinese physician. He could see the effects of Qi, but how could he account for them? That was his dilemma.

Dr. Eisenberg urged Chinese acupuncturists and Western M.D.s to open a creative dialogue to study the two divergent

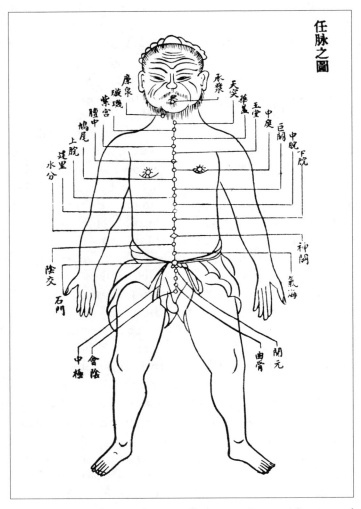

Diagram of acupuncture points on the conception meridian created during the Chinese Ming Dynasty (1368-1644).

From The True Story of Chinese Acupuncture, Vol. 1, *published by the Academy of Oriental Heritage, Vancouver, B.C., 1975. Courtesy of Henry C. Lu.*

systems, the Western mechanical model and the Chinese energy model. Might they find ways of integrating the strengths of both as part of a mindbody approach to medicine and healing?

Earlier, in 1971, American journalist James Reston described an astounding experience he had with acupuncture in China. He underwent an appendectomy with no anesthesia other than acupuncture needles strategically placed on his body surface. Chinese physicians assured him that these needles would make the pain of surgery imperceptible. They were right, as Reston excitedly reported once he got back home. Through Reston, the mystery and power of subtle energy began to enter the mainstream.

The Mystery and Power of Qigong

According to the Chinese, you can master your Qi through a series of martial arts exercises called Qigong, which literally means "energy work" or "life energy skill." Like the Five Rites, Qigong involves exercises and movements through which you learn to manipulate and control your life energy, or Qi. And as Colonel Bradford claims that the Five Rites reverse disease and illness, Qigong masters claim that Qigong eliminates major problems with prostatitis, rheumatism, colon obstructions, nervous disorders, and poor memory. Through Qigong, as well as the Five Rites, you do not gain merely ordinary good health, which is but a condition of manageable sickness; you gain robust health. Like acupuncture, Qigong is starting to come under the scrutiny of Western scientists, including Dr. Eisenberg.

Qigong has an almost supernatural aspect to it when you consider the physical marvels Qigong masters routinely perform. They often do this in public as a way of demonstrating the power of Qi. For example, in one demonstration, a man knelt on his hands and knees before a thick marble block. After taking a few special breaths, he tensed all the muscles in his body, shouted once, then slammed his forehead into the marble like a hammer—splitting the stone, not his head, in two. There was no damage at all to his forehead, not even a mark. The idea is that a Qigong master so perfectly controls his Qi that he can direct it to any part of his body, in this case his forehead.

In another demonstration, a Qigong master lay on a gymnasium floor mat with another mat laid over him, then a 1,000-pound cement slab was placed on the mat, then twelve men stood on top of the cement slab. When all of the weight was removed, there was absolutely no damage registered in the Qigong master's body. He had marshaled his Qi to his upper body to act as a buffer against the extreme weight. Another master concentrated Qi around his abdomen so that he could balance his entire body on the tines of a pitchfork. Another made his body as hard as steel by mobilizing his Qi so that a Jeep could drive over him and not leave even a nick on his skin.

To the Qigong masters such feats are not a big deal. Qi is how life works. "Emitting Qi is like exhaling for me," explained one master. "It is inside of me. It is a part of me, like an arm or a breath. Can anyone fully understand a breath?"

Not only can Qigong masters marshal internal Qi, it appears that they can also send it out of their bodies like a mechanical force. In the early 1980s, the Shanghai Institute of Traditional Chinese Medicine prepared a television documentary on Qigong. They featured a Qigong master standing before an oscilloscope. On command, he emitted Qi out of the fingers of his right hand; the oscilloscope registered the emission of Qi by making little beeps with each surge of his internal energy. "The implications were that Qi existed as a physical force and that it could be emitted at will by a Qigong master," commented Dr. Eisenberg after watching the demonstration.

Earlier in the 1970s, Chinese researchers in Hong Kong

conducted experiments on groups of people who were manipulating Qi. One group included eight Chinese physicians who projected Qi mentally to eight patients without actually touching them. Researchers noted that the temperature of the tip of the nose of each physician dropped one or two degrees during transmission of Qi while the nose-tip temperature of each patient increased by the same amount. A transfer of energy from physician to patient seemed to account for the changes in temperature.

Increasing the amount of Qi within the body is said to make an ill person robust and a weak person vibrant. According to American Qigong expert Bruce Kumar Frantzis, who trained in and out of China for 30 years, increased life energy produces improved physical health, greater mental clarity, even spiritual insight. "In fact, regular practice of Qigong exercises will lead to a body/mind that is functionally younger, so that one's 'golden years' are truly golden, rather than rusty," Frantzis says. He notes that about fifty percent of Chinese people who begin either Qigong or Tai Chi Ch'uan (another form of martial arts) do so after the age of 60 when the reality of aging is very much with them. "If a form of exercise can make the old functionally younger, its effect on the young or middle-aged is inestimable," Frantzis adds.

Frantzis's Qigong exercises are simple but effective, and include a series of full body swings, spirals, and spinal stretches. They are said to activate energy gates and circulate Qi. While his exercises don't work specifically with the chakras, and the details of his exercises are somewhat different from the Five Rites, Frantzis's swings are similar to Bradford's whirling exercise, which he said stimulates the vortex spin of all the chakras. Further, Frantzis's Qigong exercises, like the Five Rites, clearly show how physical movements, combined with mental attitude and breathing techniques, can directly affect Qi through the mindbody system and greatly improve health and longevity.

Practicing Tai Chi Ch'uan Every Day — For 120 Years

As with Qigong, Tai Chi Ch'uan is part of a Chinese system of health and longevity practices based on maximizing the circulation of life energy for improved health and rejuvenation. According to Master Da Liu, who introduced Tai Chi to the United States in the 1950s, it is a "detailed system of slow, flowing, and subtly configured motions." Like the Five Rites, it is a relaxing and toning series of exercises that releases life energy into the mindbody, and thus has numerous physiological benefits. In his late 80s, Da Liu was still teaching Tai Chi to American students.

Da Liu has a remarkable tale about his teacher, Li Ch'ing Yuen, who was born in 1678 in China. He married fourteen times, had 180 direct descendants spanning eleven generations, and lived to be 250 years old, according to Da Liu. Three years before his death in 1930, a Chinese General met Li Ch'ing Yuen and later described his physical appearance: He has good eyesight and a brisk stride; he stands seven feet tall, has very long fingernails, and a ruddy complexion. Many of Li's disciples were over 100 years old. What was the secret to his longevity? When he was 130 years old, he encountered a very old man in the mountains. This man claimed to be 500 years old and attributed his longevity to having practiced a set of exercises similar to Tai Chi Ch'uan. Called Ba-Kua, they included specific sounds, breathing instructions, dietary, and herbal recommendations. The mountain hermit taught these to Li Ch'ing Yuen and he taught them to Da Liu.

"My longevity," Master Li Ch'ing Yuen said, "is due to the fact that I performed the exercises every day—regularly, correctly, and with sincerity—for 120 years." The best time, he noted, was between 11 p.m. and 11 a.m. when he repeated each exercise two to six times. This is similar to Colonel Bradford's advice to Peter Kelder and his students: practice daily and build to 21 times for each of the Five Rites. This regularity, claimed Bradford, will produce a powerful effect that increases with time.

What shall we make of these fabulous tales? It appears that the human body has a great number of energy channels through which life energy moves and changes. Over the years, adepts in this tradition developed exercises that would maximize this energy flow and distribution for greater health, awareness, and vitality. In these traditions, whether it's China or Tibet, longevity is a science, not a gift of fate. Both the Chinese exercises and Colonel Bradford's Five Rites have us twisting and turning and stretching. They seem to compress, stimulate, and tone your acupoints, energy gates, and chakras. All of this releases dormant Qi, or prana, or life energy, much like a fountain spraying you with the precious waters of vigor and long life.

How the Five Rites Reverse Aging

Colonel Bradford and hundreds of readers who practice the Five Rites claim that these exercises reverse, or at least slow down, the aging process, and that the secret involves life energy and how one activates and uses it. But how do we account for these changes in terms that make sense to us as Westerners?

First, let's summarize the Colonel's teachings:

1. The Five Rites work according to a principle of basic life energy, or prana. This energy is the intangible, but powerful life force itself, the vital element that controls life.

2. Practicing the Five Rites regularly and in the proper sequence activates your vast reservoir of life energy, and stimulates its circulation throughout the mindbody. This creates robust health, vitality, and longevity.

3. Your life energy moves through seven "invisible" energy centers in the body called chakras, which resemble spinning vortexes or wheels.

4. The chakras work with your physical body through the seven ductless glands of the endocrine system. Life energy moves through the chakras and is distributed to the body through the endocrine glands.

5. An imbalance or shortage of any hormone secreted by the endocrine system is the result of a problem with one or more of the chakras. An endocrine system that is not functioning properly leads quickly to illness, deterioration, aging, or even death.

6. The speed of the chakra spin is the key to robust health and longevity. In a healthy person, all seven chakras spin very rapidly and at the same speed. Speed up the spin of the chakras, and you slow down the aging process. If one or more of the chakras is blocked and its natural spin is reduced or even stopped, illness and aging set in.

7. The Five Rites speed up the spinning of the chakras, coordinate their spins so they are in harmony, and distribute pure life energy to the endocrine system, and in turn to the body's organs and processes. When this happens, the result is optimal health, rejuvenation, and youthfulness.

Our brief study of the Chinese disciplines of Qigong and Tai Chi Ch'uan has shown how physical exercises, coordinated with precise knowledge of one's energy anatomy, can stimulate the circulation of Qi, literally giving us more life. Qigong exercises also work to move energy through the chakras. Anything you do to improve the circulation of Qi has to benefit the entire system. So you have a picture of basic life energy, Qi, moving through your chakras and meridians in greater amounts, thereby stimulating your internal organs and endocrine glands.

We have seen that certain traditions have developed physical exercises that enable you to activate and tap your life energy. If you practice a set of exercises like the Five Rites (or Qigong, or Tai Chi Ch'uan), designed to work with your energy centers, you will probably see profound changes in your physical, mental, and emotional well-being.

Let's take the example of the solar plexus chakra, which affects the digestion of food and is related to the liver, pancreas, stomach, gall bladder, and spleen. If you practice an exercise that affects the solar plexus chakra, over time it will have an impact on digestion and metabolism, and on all the organs and hormones involved in the assimilation of food. If your exercises are powerful, when you practice them for a long enough time they will start making major changes in the way the energy moves through this part of the body. Your digestion will improve, which means you will assimilate foods more efficiently and probably need to eat less. That means your health will improve and your vitality will increase — and that means you will look and feel better and probably younger.

You need only multiply these effects by seven to see how profoundly you can change your body when you do exercises that affect the seven chakras and all the organs and body systems they service. When you practice a set of exercises that influences the seven chakras you are accessing everything that comprises your bodily life — the circulation of energy, the organs, endocrine glands, and the biochemical links through which life energy works in your body. If your exercises make the chakras spin faster and more fully, more of this basic energy is distributed throughout your body. Whereas once the flow of energy may have been blocked, now it is open and free. Again multiply this by seven to see the cumulative effect when you work with all seven chakras.

Practicing the Five Rites creates an energy feedback loop between your physical body and its organs, the endocrine glands and their hormonal secretions, the chakra system and its energy circulation, and the source of life itself. The stretching, tightening, turning, and folding positions of the rites stimulate your endocrine glands and the seven chakras through compression and relaxation. Rite Number One (whirling) specifically speeds up the vortex spin for all seven chakras. Rite Number Two seems to work with the first five chakras from root to throat. Rite Number Three stimulates the heart and throat chakras. Rite Number Four seems to work on all seven chakras, especially as the head, containing chakras six and seven, is stretched backward and downward. Rite Number Five seems to exercise primarily the root, sacral, and two head chakras. In other words, when you practice the Five Rites, you make an energy contact with all the components of your being.

Through the Five Rites you actually massage your energy centers and indirectly, the endocrine glands they service, and through them, all your internal organs. The benefits increase the more you practice the exercises. Soon, you begin literally remaking your body from the inside out. The more you practice, the more the exercises give back to you, Colonel Bradford reminds us. "The Five Rites will help to normalize the spinning vortexes so that the body becomes even more receptive to the benefits of exercise, " explains Bradford. Is it any wonder that the Five Rites have apparently produced such dramatic results for so many people, making them look younger, feel more robust, and live longer?

There is another important point to make. Even though we identify the particular influences of one rite on one or two chakras, the set of Five Rites work together. Each exercise influences the whole system. Colonel Bradford's model comes out of a system that is holistic. The Tibetan, Hindu, and Chinese philosophies all see matter and energy, spirit and substance, psyche and body as a seamless unity, as one whole. This means that as you perform the rites over time, they have positive effects on all aspects of your being: your body looks younger, your mind thinks more clearly. You can expect heightened awareness and enhanced well-being.

It remains difficult to say precisely how each rite affects each chakra and endocrine gland as isolated influences. Even to attempt this might be a classic mistake of Western mechanistic thinking. But we can be confident that such energy exchanges and general influences are indeed possible and highly likely.

With these points made, we can turn to an additional rite Colonel Bradford described. He explained that it was desirable, but optional. This is the sixth rite.

The Sixth Rite: Conserving the Treasure of Vital Essence

The Five Rites will restore youthful health and vitality, Colonel Bradford claims. "But," he adds, "if you really want to completely restore the health and appearance of youth, there is a sixth rite which you must practice."

The sixth rite is probably the most challenging of everything Colonel Bradford taught because it attempts to rechannel sexual energy for higher purposes. To become a "superman or superwoman," celibacy or abstinence from sexual contact is required, Bradford said. The powerful life force contained in our sexual drive must be "conserved and turned upward so that it can be utilized by all the vortexes."

The Colonel had to explain this idea carefully. He was not talking about repressing the sexual drive. On the contrary, he said emphatically that unless your sexual drive is strong and vital, you cannot do the sixth rite. But here is the challenge. Once the sexual drive is alive and heightened, do not act on it. Instead, learn how to rechannel this powerful urge into the sixth rite. That is what "transmuting the active sexual urge" means. You change it, releasing its powerful energy. In this way, by "lifting it upward," sexual or reproductive energy can be transformed into longevity energy, we might say.

Bradford's sixth rite involves what Hatha yoga calls a bandha or breath-lock. You pull in the abdomen as you empty your lungs from a strong exhalation; then you hold your breath for a specified count. In yoga, bandhas are advanced practices undertaken carefully, only after preparation, and ideally, with supervision. Perhaps that's why Colonel Bradford saved teaching this rite for last. Basically, the posture of the sixth rite works with reproductive energy somewhat like a bellows. It blows the "primal heat" upwards into the higher centers away from the frenetic gravity of the first two chakras. Celibacy is required to preserve this valuable energy otherwise dissipated in sexuality. The bandha and deep breathing then use this conserved sexual energy as a kind of fuel during the performing of the sixth rite.

The average man ejaculates an estimated 5,000 times in his life. That's about 80 times a year for 65 years. This generates about four gallons of semen and anywhere between 200 to 500 million individual sperm cells per ejaculation. Over a lifetime, that is enough sperm to create one trillion human lives. From an energy viewpoint, this is an awesome creative force. Imagine what you could do with this energy if you used it differently. You could probably live longer, for one. "In a very real sense, every man can create a stockpile of sexual energy literally more potent than the atomic bomb," noted well-known Taoist author Mantak Chia.

This is the idea behind the sixth rite: If you're celibate, you can conserve your powerful reproductive energy and rechannel it to create maximum health, rejuvenation, and longevity. But the Colonel knew that a celibate life was simply not a feasible choice for many people, so he recommended putting it off until you are truly ready to take on this difficult challenge.

The Importance of Believing You Can Be Younger

In addition to the six rites, Colonel Bradford offers a recommendation that is just as important as the exercises. You have to believe it is possible to halt or at least minimize the effects of the aging process, and you have to believe that you can actually do it. This mental attitude makes all the difference. "If you are able to see yourself as young, in spite of your age, others will see you that way, too," explains Colonel Bradford.

It's really a form of magic, smoke and mirrors, except the primary audience is your disbelieving self. Bradford told his students that when he began practicing the rites in Tibet, he saw himself as a younger man. Rather than dwelling on the supposed reality of himself as a "feeble old man," he remembered himself when he had been "in the prime of life." He invested psychic energy and "very strong desire" every day in an image of his youthful self. Gradually he began to see himself looking younger, as that virile young man. And so did all those who met him.

You've probably heard expressions like these: *It's all in your mind. You create your own reality. It's mind over matter. She willed it to be.* Is there some kind of hocus pocus behind these concepts? Or are they accurate reflections of some fundamental reality?

While modern science strives to separate the mind and physical matter, portraying them as unrelated phenomena, Eastern philosophies teach just the opposite. They see all matter as the product of consciousness. Consciousness is the first principle of creation, the stuff out of which matter is made. Matter is consciousness congealed or coalesced.

In the 20th century, quantum physics is showing us validity in the Eastern view. Scientists are slowly coming around to the notion that perhaps one's awareness does affect matter. Some are even drafting new models of "vibrational medicine" and "quantum healing." If consciousness is indeed the raw material from which matter is made, it's reasonable to conclude that your thoughts shape your physical reality (your body), and mold its behavior (your health).

Deepak Chopra, M.D., explains this new view of matter by combining the mystical insights of meditation, the theories of modern physics, and his own experiences as a practicing physician. As Chopra sees it, we live in a flux of potentialities that are given shape and substance by mind. Reality is unrestricted and evolving. It could be almost anything.

This is true even at the level of the electron. We used to think that an electron was like a little planet spinning around the nucleus of an atom; it was predictable, always there for us to perceive. But today physicists think that this traditional view of an electron exists only when we observe it as such. In truth, they say, the electron does not exist anywhere; it is potentially everywhere. It is our view of the electron that gives it definition. In other words, *as it is seen, so it is.* Once again, we're reminded that one of the keys to Bradford's success in creating a younger body was seeing himself as younger.

The phenomenon called the *placebo effect* vividly demonstrates that your expectations and beliefs can directly affect your physical condition. A placebo is nothing more than a sugar pill given to patients who believe that they are receiving a beneficial drug. Roughly one-third of the patients who receive a placebo experience improvement, just as if they had taken an active drug. Presumably it is the patient's mind and its expectation of improvement that has created actual physical improvement.

The work of Los Angeles psychotherapist Evelyn Silvers,

Ph.D. shows how powerful the placebo effect can be. She told subjects suffering from chronic pain that their bodies house an "inner pharmacy." Using a combination of suggestion and guided visualization, she encouraged patients to stimulate the production of pain-killing "drugs." She asked them to imagine that they were building up a large supply of endorphins (the body's natural pain killers), which they could then mentally inject into the bloodstream. The results were impressive. Using this technique, many patients were able to eliminate or reduce chronic pain and wean themselves from addictive painkillers. Later, Dr. Silvers used a similar technique to help drug addicts kick the habit after 4 to 40 years of drug dependency.

"I find this a superb example of how awareness can heal," notes Dr. Chopra. "Once a plausible tool was offered, the mind allowed itself to break out of an old boundary." The brain is a neutral agent with no will of its own, says Chopra. It is an "infinitely resourceful servant" which can accept or reject any addiction. By addiction, Chopra also means the fixed belief that the aging process and physical decline cannot be stopped.

According to Chopra, self is the supreme master. Long life will be ours if we think it possible. His philosophy helps explain why Colonel Bradford emphasizes the importance of desire, attitude, and belief for those who wish to overcome aging and decline.

Scientists Study Life Energy

Energy and its effects are at the heart of Colonel Bradford's Five Rites for attaining the fountain of youth. Can this elusive but powerful energy current called prana or Qi be seen, measured, and quantified by scientists? Does energy actually have a primary role in health, illness, and healing as the Chinese acupuncturists claim? Is there current scientific proof for the

Eastern claims about energy? Despite considerable resistance from doctors and scientists entrenched in their view of matter and reality, there is.

What perhaps opened the door most recently to this unseen world of energy was the emergence in the 1980s of high technology medical imaging devices that record electromagnetic energy fields surrounding individual bodily organs and the entire body as a whole. Scientists are now able to take pictures of the minutely detectable electromagnetic fields.

Devices such as Magnetic Resonance Imaging (MRI) and others now offer physicians a computerized sensing system to obtain pictures of the brain and other organs. MRIs are now used widely in hospitals and laboratories across the country as a valuable diagnostic tool.

Then there is the ground-breaking research of radiologist Dr. Bjorn Nordenstrom at the Karolinska Institute in Sweden. Nordenstrom contends that the body has a system of electric circuits and that electrical activity may be the basis of the healing process. His work has shown that an electrical current that flows through the body may, when strengthened, stop cancer cell growth. The body's electrical system, Nordenstrom maintains, is as critical to human health as blood circulation.

Recent developments in the field of acupuncture have broken new ground in the quest to prove invisible energy. A German acupuncturist named Dr. Reinhard Voll invented a device called the Dermatron and a technique called electroacupuncture. The physician uses a computer to monitor the electrical valve of any acupoint in the body. The computer displays the electrical readings before and during an acupuncture treatment to guide the physician.

A Japanese researcher named Dr. Hiroshi Motoyama developed the AMI Machine (Apparatus for Measuring the Functions of the Meridians and Corresponding Internal Organs), also used with acupoints on the skin. The AMI has 28 electrodes that the doctor attaches to acupoints, usually on the fingers and toes. A computer collects electrical data received by the AMI. Through this approach, Motoyama found that there are strong connections between electrically imbalanced meridians and underlying disease conditions in the related organs. "Experiments on some 2,000 subjects strongly suggest that the relative magnitudes of such skin current values reflect the functional conditions of Qi energy in the meridians," Motoyama reported.

Dr. Motoyama also invented a chakra instrument that detects minute energy changes emitted by the body or regions of the body associated with the different chakras. He reasoned that insofar as the chakras are related to the nervous system ganglia and the corresponding organs, changes in electrical state, produced by a person's activities or thoughts, should be detectable by this instrument. His data led him to this startling conclusion: "Psi energy (Qi) working in the chakras can extinguish or create energy in the physical dimension." In other words, Qi in the chakras directly affects the quality and health of our physical organs, and Motoyama had the scientific measurements to prove it.

Motoyama, Voll, and Nordenstrom are only a few among the many scientists and researchers who are now studying the human energy field. They're teaching us about its anatomy, its energy channels, and the relationship of all this to health, illness, healing, and aging. They're giving us new ways of interacting with this energy domain at the heart of our lives. Quite likely, the results of this research will support and deepen Colonel Bradford's teachings. Surely it will help us as Westerners interested in the Five Rites to deepen our understanding of the biochemistry and energy mechanisms that make longevity possible. We may well conclude, as Colonel Bradford did, but with more scientific understanding, that the fountain of youth was always within us.

In the meantime, if we insist that everything Bradford claims to be true must be scientifically proven, we may be disappointed. Science doesn't have all the tools and concepts needed to do the job. Still we need not take the claims in *Ancient Secret of the Fountain of Youth* entirely on faith. As we've seen, Colonel Bradford is not the only one making dramatic claims about remarkable longevity. Great and long-standing traditions stand behind these claims. The secrets and powers of life force energy have been thoroughly explored in China, India, and Tibet, among other cultures. What seems a secret to most of us is common sense, even standard knowledge for many in those cultures. If you learn nothing else from this brief visit with Eastern cultures, for whom energy is as tangible as your hand, it is that direct experience is the best proof. Were Bradford still with us he might well say something like this: "Probe the energy secrets if you wish, but by all means practice the Five Rites and see for yourself."

If you're familiar with yoga, you'll see that the Five Rites and yoga are similar in many ways. Over the years, questions regarding the link between yoga and the Five Rites have come up again and again. In the next chapter, we'll explore this important relationship. Questions regarding how to do the Five Rites most effectively have also been asked again and again. In the next chapter we'll answer these questions and focus on the exercises themselves in greater detail.

Richard Leviton has been a natural health journalist for 20 years, having been Senior Writer for East West Journal (now Natural Health), Yoga Journal, and The Quest. He is the author of numerous books including The Imagination of Pentecost *(Anthroposophic Press, 1994),* Brain Builders *(Prentice Hall, 1995), and* Looking for Arthur *(Station Hill Press, 1995). Richard is currently Executive Editor of* Alternative Medicine Digest *and Future Medicine Publishing.*

CHAPTER FIVE

The Five Rites and Yoga:
Exercises for Renewed Health and Longevity

by Jeff Migdow, M.D.
as told to Laura Faye Taxel

The five Tibetan rites presented in *Ancient Secret of the Fountain of Youth* can be described as a modified version of Hatha yoga postures. It's clear to me that the two spring from the same source. Both the Five Rites and Hatha yoga are based on a similar understanding of the human body and how it works.

Yoga is an ancient science, not a religion, that enables one to unite the body, mind, and spirit; the word itself means union. Westerners might use the word wholeness to describe the concept. Yogic postures are designed to heal and revitalize the body, calm the emotions, and clear the mind, and they can be done solely for this purpose. However, meditation is considered the real end product of practice.

To meditate is to make an intentional effort to be quiet, calm, and aware. It can expand and enhance perceptions of another level of reality, no matter what belief system you may ascribe to. Whether you think of it as prayer, contemplation, or the quest for consciousness, meditation is a kind of deep and silent process of observation that makes it possible to experience a sense of being present. I describe presence as an intense feeling of being in touch with what's going on in and around myself. For me, the daily practice of yoga and meditation has meant that I am more connected to whatever I'm doing in the moment. I feel alive, positive, and able to experience meaning in my life.

Yoga practices are specifically designed to create the physical relaxation and mental tranquillity necessary to achieve this higher quality of life. The exercises are a method for "yoking" together the physical with the mental and spiritual parts of a human being so they can serve one another and function in harmony. The postures actually lead those who do them into a meditative state.

They also help build up the physical strength and stamina necessary for the practice of a meditative spiritual discipline. *Prana*, a Hindu term used by those who practice yoga, means both energy and spirit. The two are inextricably intertwined. The Greeks, too, made the same connection: pneuma meant breath and also spirit. Consider the single, simple fact that to meditate, it's essential to sit very still and upright for a long period of time. Most people in today's world are too nervous, too stiff, and too tired to be able to do this for more than a few minutes. Yogic postures train and prepare the body to sit still and cross-legged with the spine straight and unsupported. In *tantric literature* (religious writings), it is written that the Buddha himself once said, "Without a perfectly healthy body, one cannot know bliss."

In recent years modern science has begun to document and verify the beneficial psychological and physiological effects of yoga, meditation, and yoga-like practices such as the Five Rites.

A study published in *Journal of Research In Indian Medicine* found that the daily practice of yoga asanas (postures) for six months led to a decreased heart rate, a drop in blood pressure, weight loss, a lower breathing rate accompanied by an increase in lung capacity and chest expansion, and a decline in incidence of anxiety. A subsequent study found that regular yoga practice led to a decrease in physiological stress, lower cholesterol levels, balanced blood sugar levels, an increase in alpha brain waves (associated with relaxation), and a general reduction of physical problems.

Numerous other studies have produced similar results. T. J. Thorpe, Ph.D., of the University of Tennessee, found that yoga practitioners consistently reported decreases in feelings of anxiety and nervousness. Many of his subjects experienced relief from symptoms of insomnia, fatigue, headaches, body aches, spinal curvature, dizziness, joint stiffness, and skin problems. Yoga was helpful for those dealing with obesity, and some noticed a decrease in the use of alcohol and cigarettes. Benefits included an increase in feelings of composure, relaxation, and joy, improvements in interpersonal relationships, and an increased capacity for concentration.

In another experiment, Dr. V. H. Dhanaraj of the University of Alberta, in Canada, compared a group of people who engaged in six weeks of yoga practice with a group that did conventional exercises for the same period. He found that those who practiced yoga showed significantly greater improvements in cell metabolism, oxygen consumption and lung capacity, cardiac efficiency, thyroid function, hemoglobin and red blood cell count, and overall flexibility.

From India to Tibet:
The Historical Link Between Yoga and the Five Rites

Scholars believe that a Buddhist master named Milarepa brought yoga to Tibet from India sometime in the 11th or 12th century A.D. It's my understanding that, in those ancient times, as well as today, Tibetan people did not see their spiritual lives as separate from their day-to-day existence. They believed that the presence of God could be felt in their own vitality. They experimented with practices that helped them connect their physical bodies with their spiritual selves, their souls. My feeling is that the Tibetan monks discovered over time what was, for them, an effective combination of yoga exercises which became what we call the Five Rites. The rugged, mountainous conditions they lived in may well account for their particular emphasis on vigor.

The Five Rites are quite special in that I think they represent a very old teaching that has come to us intact. By contrast, most of the yoga sequences that are being taught in the West today have been created within the past 50 years. The meditation techniques and postures are ancient, but the ways of practicing them are often modern adaptations. Traditionally these postures and exercises were passed on orally, from teacher to student, and they were constantly being modified and recreated. But I believe the form and sequence of the Five Rites are centuries old. Therefore, I think it's very important to do the rites as they're presented, without altering the form and sequence. The order makes sense to me from the perspective of my medical training and my personal experiences practicing both yoga and the rites. And the fact that people continue to find this sequence effective and get beneficial results makes the best case of all for not changing the manner in which they're done.

A Body Blueprint: The Master Plan for Energy Flow

According to the systems of thought in which both yoga and the rites are rooted, human beings have a number of energy centers. In yoga they're called *chakras* and the Tibetan monks described them as vortexes. Specific movements can stimulate and "open" these energy centers (see Chapter Four).

According to the principles of yoga, the chakras are not actually located in the physical body. They comprise what's called the energy body, an energy field that surrounds your physical self. But they correspond to precise points within the body where our life energy flows into the nervous system.

Those who practice and understand yoga believe that not only do we produce energy in our bodies, but we also receive energy from outside ourselves. Other cultures and healing philosophies include similar references: the Chinese call this essential and subtle energy *Qi* (pronounced chee). And in *Ancient Secret of the Fountain of Youth*, Colonel Bradford uses the Hindu term prana (vital life energy). (For a detailed discussion of the chakras, see Chapter Four.)

To Western minds, the idea of invisible chakras and subtle energy may seem strange at first. But is it any stranger than the way a television works? A satellite dish set up outdoors picks up invisible electromagnetic waves. We can't see those waves rippling through the air but we know they're there. When the whole system's working properly, they're translated into vivid pictures and sounds on TV screens.

Similarly, chakras are like the satellite dishes that "catch" needed energy. In fact, according to Peter Kelder's account, the Tibetan monks taught the Colonel that the vortexes represent powerful electrical fields. When they're in balance, or spinning at a normal rate of speed, vital life energy flows through our system as it should.

Indeed, science has confirmed that this ancient system of physiology is rooted in biological fact. We now know that bundles of nerves, called *plexi*, are actually located at the site of each chakra. These plexi are part of the sympathetic nervous system, which helps energize and stimulate our organs and glands. This is the "activating" system that, for example, tells the heart to beat and the lungs to expand and contract.

Two Paths to a Healthy Lifestyle

While there are many similarities between the practice of yoga and the Five Rites, there are also contrasts. It seems to me that the Five Rites offer a simpler, more practical way to reap the rewards of yoga and enjoy its benefits every day. The rites are less daunting than yoga, and when described clearly, they can be self-taught, making them easier to learn and follow than the unfamiliar and often difficult postures of traditional yoga. The rites are appealing because they involve repetitive movements, much like the kind of exercise routines most of us are familiar with. They require only a small commitment of time, and people find that attractive, too.

But it's important to understand that the rites and the practice of yoga are not in competition with one another. I don't want to say that one is better than the other. They are related, they are different, and they can effectively complement one another.

Some people may actually find the Five Rites more difficult to do than yoga, especially at first. They can be challenging. You need muscle strength and a certain level of flexibility and balance to do them properly. A good way to begin is to do basic yoga postures, which, for the most part, are held for only twenty seconds, as a warm-up for the more strenuous rites.

The Inside Story:
What Yoga and the Five Rites Do for Your Body

Both yoga and the Five Rites, practiced independently or in combination, have a definite rejuvenating effect on those who do them regularly. From a medical point of view, it's easy to understand why.

CIRCULATION: THE KEY TO GOOD HEALTH

The exercises directly and positively affect circulation. Improved circulation speeds the healing process and gives the immune system a boost. More blood is pumped with fewer heartbeats, so there is less stress on the heart. When the flow of blood is improved, every cell in the body receives more oxygen and nutrients, and waste products are washed away more efficiently.

REJUVENATION, CELL BY CELL

Oxygen, sugar, and nutrients provide the fuel cells need to make energy. This fuel is carried to the cells by the blood. As cells make energy, they give off carbon dioxide, the waste they've got to get rid of. This is actually respiration and digestion on a cellular level. When we breathe, we take in oxygen and breathe out carbon dioxide. When we eat, we take in nutrients and eliminate what we don't need.

Visualize each cell in your body as a tiny factory. Better circulation, or blood flow, means more fuel and "spare parts" arriving all the time, so energy production stays high. The blood also acts as a conveyor belt, carrying away waste and debris more efficiently as circulation improves.

It's my view that this cellular rejuvenation could account for some of the "miraculous" changes people say the rites have generated, like the darkening of gray hair or the return of hair growth, profoundly new feelings of well-being and vitality, and smoother, younger-looking skin.

RELAXATION: THE REAL ROAD TO RENEWAL

It's important to understand the critical importance of relaxation in conjunction with any form of physical exertion, be it aerobic or isometric exercise, yoga, or the Five Rites. Exercise and vigorous yogic practices such as the Five Rites tend to increase muscle tension because of the great mental effort and physical exertion involved in these activities. While increased muscle tension brings extra blood to your muscles, it also decreases the flow of blood to vital organs. This increases the risk of injury, high blood pressure, anxiety, and stress on your heart. Therefore, it is essential to warm up prior to exertion, and to relax afterward to minimize muscle tension.

Relaxation before and after exertion, including the Five Rites, allows the muscles to relax, increasing blood flow to vital organs. Make sure you give yourself time to relax before and after practicing the Five Rites so that the physical, mental, and spiritual benefits aren't negated by excess tension. Through relaxation, the benefits of doing the Five Rites will be greatly enhanced!

If you enjoy aerobic and/or isometric exercise, I recommend that you practice the Five Rites or yoga in addition to your usual exercise routine. If you have no formal exercise program, you can view the Five Rites and yoga as a beneficial and complete approach to exercise.

A WHOLE BODY WORKOUT

Most Western-style exercise routines affect only certain parts of the body. A series of yoga postures or the Five Rites are designed to affect every part of the body, every energy center, organ, and system. For example, the rites cause the body to go against gravity. This stimulates the development of osteoblasts (cells that promote bone growth). In studies done with women in their 70s, it was found that if they simply walked four times a week for 20 minutes, a mildly antigravity activity, osteoporosis (bone deterioration) slowed down to almost premenopausal levels. Imagine how much gain could be achieved with the practice of yoga and/or the Five Rites, which involve the entire body in repetitive movements against gravity.

Another way in which both yoga and the rites impact the

body systemically is by massaging the internal organs. Pressing, squeezing, and then letting go, as you do in Rites Two, Four, and Five, stimulates the release of toxins and old blood from the organs of the digestive system, as it brings in fresh blood which literally washes away these impurities. This in turn encourages healthy digestion and elimination. Rites Three and Five have a similar effect on the lungs, cleansing the muscles related to breathing in the chest and the diaphragm and giving them a good workout. Breathing will be deeper and freer, even when you are no longer exercising, which I think explains, in part, why those who do the rites notice they feel generally better throughout the day.

The Five Rites

Before you begin to practice the Five Rites, here are some important things you should know:

1. For the first week, perform each of the Five Rites three times, once a day. Then, each week for nine weeks, add two more repetitions of each rite. At the end of nine weeks, you'll be doing 21 repetitions of each. If you need to increase the number of repetitions at a slower pace, that's fine. It's best to do the rites in the morning, so the beneficial effects extend into your day. If you wish, you can do the entire sequence twice a day, morning and evening but there's no need to do more than 21 in order to achieve the desired results.

2. Practice the rites according to directions. Any change dilutes their effect. Even if you are quite physically fit and

capable of more repetitions, do only the prescribed number. If you're looking for additional challenge, do the rites more quickly or add another type of workout or exercise routine to your day. The major benefits of the Five Rites come from movements that quicken and balance the spinning of the body's energy centers.

3. There will inevitably be days in your life when you are unable to perform the entire routine; you may be ill or just too busy. Doing just three of each rite, which takes only about two minutes, is much better than not doing any at all.

4. Any type of exercise that's new for the body must be undertaken with care. Doing the rites can set many physical changes in motion. Initially, the rites, which stimulate circulation, can have a dramatic detoxifying effect, and that's one reason for working into the full routine gradually. Once you begin, you may notice that your urine is a darker color or has a strong odor. It may sting or burn when you urinate. Women might develop a vaginal infection. You may notice an unpleasant change in the smell of your sweat or a slight rash on the skin. You might develop a slight upper respiratory infection or discomfort in your joints. All these symptoms are normal, temporary, and even desirable. They are physical manifestations of the poisons and pollutants which have been stored and now are being excreted from organs, joints, and mucous membranes. But to be sure these symptoms do not require medical attention and are not the result of an unrelated health problem, consult with your doctor.

Once you are certain that these symptoms are, in fact, the result of the detoxification process, give them a week to pass. Don't try to relieve them with medication. Detoxification is a key to feeling better. If your reaction seems very strong to you, cut back to fewer repetitions of each rite, or do each rite at a much slower rate. It also helps to drink more water than you usually do to flush out your system.

Some dietary changes could also be useful. Cut back on your consumption of dairy products, beef, pork, fats, sugar, bread, coffee and other products containing caffeine. If you smoke, it's very helpful to cut back by at least one-half. In fact, doing the Five Rites is a wonderful way to help you stop smoking completely! Consume more fresh fruits and vegetables and whole grains. Within a short time, you should begin to feel energized and healthier. Your eyes will be clearer, your skin brighter, and your limbs more flexible.

Getting Ready: Warm-ups, Stretches, and Strengtheners

I've created a routine of yoga-style exercises that can be done prior to the Five Rites as a warm-up and to further enhance their rejuvenating effects. Some of these postures and exercises correspond to specific rites. If you're having difficulty with a particular rite, the warm-up can help you develop the strength and flexibility you need to do it. Many of these stretches can be done throughout the day. If you have a condition that precludes your doing one or more of the rites, you may do the corresponding warm-up instead (see "Using Warm-ups as Alternatives" on page 140). Some are actual yoga postures. Others, based upon the principles of yoga, were invented by me or other yoga teachers. The entire sequence takes only about 8 to 10 minutes to complete.

These warm-ups, stretches, and body strengtheners release excess tension, which can help prevent injury and focus the mind on the body. This will help you do the rites more easily, effectively, and with less chance of strain. They are gentle, safe movements, and are not too difficult for most people to do regardless of age or physical condition. They are meant to be relaxing.

I suggest you do these stretches and warm-ups in the order in which I've given them here, since the sequence is designed as the optimal preparation for the rites. You can choose to do all of them, or select the ones you feel you need, but don't change the progression. Always do your warm-ups before doing the rites. (Before beginning each warm-up, you might want to quickly read over the directions so you understand the sequence of movements ahead of time.)

Body Scan with Abdominal Breathing

- Lie flat on your back with your arms resting on the floor, palms facing up. Breathe in and out slowly and deeply several times.

- Keeping your shoulders and buttocks in place, breathe in and press your abdomen upward lifting the small of your back off the floor.

- Then breathe out, releasing your abdominal muscles so that the small of your back returns to a resting position on the floor.

- As you do the exercise, mentally scan your body. Starting at your head and slowly working your way down, visit each part of the body, briefly focusing your attention there.

- Each time you breathe in, become aware of tension and other sensations in the area where your attention is focused.

- Each time you breathe out, release any tension you find and relax the area completely.

- Repeat, spending about 2 minutes on this sequence.

Spinal Rocking

Spinal Rocking releases tension from your back.

- Lying flat on your back, hug your knees to your chest by clasping your hands together under the fold of your knees.

- Bring your chin to your chest, curve your spine, and rock back so that your shoulder blades come down to the floor. Then rock forward so that your tailbone comes down to the floor.

- Breathing normally, continue to rock back and forth several times.

- In addition to, or in place of the above exercise, you may do the following:

- When you hug your knees to your chest, slowly rock your legs sideways back and forth several times. Breathe normally, and try to keep your back flat on the floor.

- Continue the rocking for 15 to 20 seconds.

Bridge Warm-Up

The Bridge Warm-Up builds strength for Rite Number Four, and, if necessary, can be done in its place. It releases tension from the lower back and pelvis.

- Lie flat on your back with your arms on the floor, palms facing down. Bending your legs at the knees, plant your feet on the floor near the buttocks.

- Breathe in as you slowly press your pelvis up a few inches off the floor.

- Breathe out as you slowly release and lower your pelvis to the original position.

- Do this 10 times.

Abdominal Strengthener

The Abdominal Strengthener builds strength for Rite Number Two, and,
if necessary, can be done in its place.

◆ Recline on the floor with your legs extended, and elevate your head
and shoulders by propping yourself up on your elbows. Your forearms
should be flat on the floor, palms facing down.

◆ Breathe in as you lift both legs about 6 inches off the floor. Keeping
your legs as straight as possible, continue to hold them off the floor for
10 to 20 seconds, if you can. While you are holding your legs up, breathe
in and out normally. Keep your eyes open, and look at your toes.

◆ Breathe out as you lower your legs to a resting position on the floor.
Pause.

◆ Do this 3 to 5 times to strengthen abdominal muscles.

Leg Bangers

Leg Bangers release tension in your legs and tone the thighs.

◆ Recline on the floor just as you did in the beginning position for the Abdominal Strengthener.

◆ Flexing your legs at the knees, rhythmically bang them up and down against the floor. Bang first one leg and then the other in rapid succession. Your heels should remain in contact with the floor.

◆ Breathe in and out normally, keep your eyes open, and look at your legs.

◆ Do this for 15 to 20 seconds.

Table with Cat and Dog

Table with Cat and Dog is useful for releasing tension in your back and hips, and toning these areas.

- Get down on the floor on your hands and knees with your hands positioned under your shoulders and your knees positioned under your hips. This is often called the table position.

- Breathe in as you allow your back to sag. At the same time, bring your chin up and rotate your pelvis so that the tailbone moves up. This is the dog position.

- Breathe out as you arch your back upward. At the same time, tuck your chin to your chest, and rotate your pelvis so that the tailbone moves down. This is the cat position.

- Repeat the entire sequence 3 times.

Puppy Stretch

- Begin in the table position as described in the first step of Table with Cat and Dog.

- Without moving your hands or knees, bend at the hips and sink backwards, so that your buttocks are resting on your ankles.

- Breathe out as you bring your chin to your chest.

- Breathe in as you stretch your hands in front of you as far as they will go, all the while keeping your palms down on the floor. Hold this position for 15 seconds, breathing slowly and deeply.

- Release and return to the starting position.

- Do this only once.

Downward Dog

The Downward Dog is a good preparation for Rite Number Five and, if necessary, can be done in its place.

- Begin in the table position.

- Curl your toes under, and breathe in as you bend at your hips, raising your buttocks so that your body forms an inverted V, just as it does in Rite Number Five. Your knees will lift up off the floor, your legs will be straight, and your outstretched arms will be in a straight line with your back. Hold this position for 15 seconds, breathing slowly and deeply.

- Breathe out as you return to the table position.

- Do this only once.

Rag Doll

- From a relaxed standing position, bend at the hips as if you were bending down to touch your toes.

- In this position, allow your torso, head, and arms to hang limply. You should feel loose and relaxed. Your legs may be straight or slightly bent at the knees.

- Remain in this position for 15 to 20 seconds, and then slowly return to a standing position.

- Do this only once.

Helicopter

The Helicopter releases tension in your upper back, shoulders, and neck, helping to prevent neck and shoulder strain. It is good preparation for Rite Number One, and, if necessary, can be done in its place.

- Begin in a standing position, feet planted firmly on the floor about 12 inches apart. Keep your eyes opened.

- Extend your arms straight out from your sides, palms down, until your arms are level with your shoulders.

- Pivot the trunk of your body so that your extended arms swing back and forth rhythmically. Keep your arms loose, relax your spine, and give in to the swinging movement.

- As you swing your arms to the right, allow your left hand to slap against your right shoulder while the back of your right hand slaps against the small of your back.

- As you swing your arms in the opposite direction, allow your right hand to slap against your left shoulder while the back of your left hand slaps against the small of your back.

- As you swing back and forth, allow your torso and legs to follow through with the movement. Lift your left heel as you swing right. Lift your right heel as you swing left. But don't allow either foot to completely leave the floor.

- As you swing to the right, turn your head left, and as you swing back to the left, turn your head right.

- Breathe in rhythm with your swinging movement.

- Repeat for 20 swings.

Head Rolls

Head Rolls open and relax your throat, neck area, upper back, and shoulders. They help prevent neck strain.

- Stand upright in a relaxed position. Breathe in deeply.

- Breathe out slowly as you gently tilt your head sideways toward your right shoulder. Hold 5 seconds.

- Breathe in as you return your head to an upright position.

- Breathe out as you gently lower your head forward, chin to chest. Hold 5 seconds.

- Breathe in as you return your head to an upright position.

- Breathe out as you gently tilt your head sideways toward your left shoulder. Hold 5 seconds.

- Breathe in as you again return your head to an upright position.

- Breathe out as you gently recline your head backward. Hold 5 seconds.

- Breathe in as you return your head to an upright position.

- Do this sequence of movements only once.

Shoulder Rolls

Shoulder Rolls help you to relax and let go, releasing tension in the shoulder and upper back area and preventing shoulder strain.

- Stand upright with your body relaxed and your arms hanging loosely at your sides. Breathe normally.

- Slowly roll or rotate your shoulders in a forward circular motion 5 times.

- Then, reverse the movement, slowly rotating your shoulders in a backward circular motion 5 times.

- Finally, take several deep breaths, sighing as you breathe out fully.

Spider Push-Ups

Spider Push-Ups strengthen the wrists and can help prevent wrist strain. They build wrist strength necessary for Rites Number Four and Five.

- Stand upright with your arms held up, elbows bent, hands together in front of your chest, and forearms more or less level with the floor.

- Spread your fingers apart, and, with the palms of your hands facing, touch the finger tips of one hand against the corresponding fingertips of the other hand.

- Press inward on your fingers until their inside surfaces are mostly touching. Your knuckles will be flexed in a convex curve. The palms of your hands will not be touching one another.

- Release, and then press your fingers together again. You are now doing push-ups.

- Slowly do 10 push-ups with your eyes opened, watching your hands.
  Breathe normally.

Wrist Squeeze

The Wrist Squeeze strengthens the wrists and can help prevent wrist strain and Carpal Tunnel Syndrome. The Squeeze strengthens your wrists for Rites Number Four and Five.

- In a relaxed, standing position, hold your left forearm upright with the palm of your left hand in front of your face. Breathe normally.

- Clasp your right hand around your left wrist, with your right thumb resting against the inside of the wrist.

- Squeeze gently but firmly 10 times.

- Repeat the procedure with the left hand squeezing the right wrist.

Thigh Strengthener

The Thigh Strengthener is good preparation for Rite Number Three, and, if necessary, can be done in its place.

- Stand in front of a wall, facing away from it. Your feet should be about 6 inches apart, and your heels should be 12 to 18 inches from the wall.

- Without moving your feet, bend slightly at the hips, and lean back until your buttocks rest against the wall.

- Breathe in. Then, breathe out as you slide downward, bending your knees as you go, and keeping your buttocks in contact with the wall. Continue sliding, until your thighs are in a horizontal position, just as if you were sitting upright in an invisible chair.

- Flatten your back against the wall so that your spine contacts the wall, top to bottom. Breathe in and out deeply.

- Hold this position as long as you can up to 15 seconds. If you're in the correct posture, your thighs should quiver.

- Breathe in as you slide back up. Take a few deep breaths before repeating.

- Do the entire sequence 2 or 3 times.

After doing these warm-ups, rest for a minute or two to help relax your system before beginning the Five Rites.

Using Warm-ups as Alternatives to the Five Rites

If you have a condition that makes it impossible to do a particular rite or if your health care practitioner advises against it, you can do the corresponding recommended warm-up exercise instead.

- For Rite Number One substitute the HELICOPTER.

- For Rite Number Two substitute the ABDOMINAL STRENGTHENER.

- For Rite Number Three substitute the THIGH STRENGTHENER.

- For Rite Number Four substitute the BRIDGE WARM-UP.

- For Rite Number Five substitute the DOWNWARD DOG.

A Step-By-Step Guide to Doing the Five Rites

With sufficient time, patience, and effort, most people, no matter what their age or physical condition, are able to do the Five Rites well enough to enjoy the health benefits they bring. Not everyone can do all of them at first, or do them perfectly. If you are unable to do a particular rite, substitute the warm-up I've described. If even that is impossible for you, continue to do those rites you are able to do, and come back to the others or their substitutes when you are ready.

Some medical conditions might preclude your doing certain rites. I've included a short list of those conditions following the instructions for each rite. If you have any of the conditions listed, I suggest you seek a doctor's advice before beginning. The lists are by no means comprehensive. If you have any diagnosed disease or physical handicap and are under a professional's care, discuss the rites with your health care practitioner before you start doing them.

While performing the rites, strive to breathe slowly, deeply and evenly. There is a direct link between the quality of breathing and the benefits the Five Rites can deliver. Most people use only two-thirds of their lung capacity. Deep breathing cleanses the lungs, replacing stale air with fresh air, and getting more oxygen into the bloodstream. Oxygenated blood is what revitalizes and re-energizes the cells. Slower breathing also optimizes the heart's pumping ability, thus improving circulation so that the oxygenated blood is effectively brought to each and every cell in the body.

Rite Number One

Rite Number One requires special explanation. Unlike the others, it does not resemble a traditional yoga posture or exercise, but it is a special technique that appears in many esoteric and spiritual disciplines. The emphasis is on movement rather than posture, and it involves spinning to stimulate the flow of energy in the body. A branch of the *Sufis*, a mystical Islamic sect, are known as whirling dervishes because of their practice of spinning to induce a heightened state of consciousness.

In her best-selling book, *Mutant Message Down Under*, Marlo Morgan relates the astonishing fact that the aborigines of Australia also regard spinning as a means to stimulate the flow of life energy. Living for a period of months in the outback with a small band of aborigines, Morgan was taught that there are seven key energy centers in the body and that energy could be increased in each one by spinning. She even uses the word vortexes to describe these centers.

I think spinning happens naturally, which is why it appears as a form of movement in so many different cultures. It happens spontaneously to yogis when their energy level gets very high, and it's a way to channel this energy throughout the nervous system. It can produce feelings of bliss and I have read that for the Sufi, it is a manifestation of ecstasy. But on a simpler level, spinning feels good. It's fun and I think that's why children like to do it. I've noticed, too, that when my daughter Kelly spins when playing, she tends to do it in a clockwise manner. The direction is significant; it's the way the chakras "want" to go.

HELPS RELIEVE
* Varicose veins
* Osteoporosis
* Headaches

HEALTH BENEFITS
Rite Number One enhances circulation, which in turn can help alleviate varicose veins; tones the arms and can help if you have osteoporosis in the arms; increases the energy flow through all the chakras, especially those located in the top of the head, the forehead, the chest, and the knees, stimulating revitalization of the cells; aids the flow of cerebral-spinal fluid which contributes to mental clarity and helps prevent headaches. Doing Rite Number One daily can spark a process of rejuvenation for the entire body.

Rite Number One

Starting Position

◆ Stand erect with arms outstretched, horizontal to the floor, palms facing down. Shoulders should not be hunched or tense, and your arms should be in line with your shoulders.

◆ Picture a clock on the floor, under your feet, face up. When you begin to spin, turn in the same direction as the hands of the clock.

Action

◆ Turn from left to right, spinning around in a complete circle. Begin and end slowly, building up speed and decelerating gradually. This prevents undue stress on the body. Breathe slowly and evenly as you spin.

◆ You may become slightly dizzy. To alleviate this, focus your vision on a single point straight ahead of you before you begin spinning. As you turn, keep your eyes on that point as long as possible. When this point enters your field of vision again, refocus on it.

◆ When you are finished spinning, take a few deep breaths, breathing in and out through the nose. Relax your body. Lie down in preparation for Rite Number Two. Wait for any lingering dizziness to disappear. Do not begin the next rite until you feel completely back in balance.

TIPS

- Let your feet follow your arms.
- Try not to wander as you spin. Finish spinning in approximately the same place in the room where you began.
- Keep your chin parallel to the ground, your shoulders relaxed.

IF YOU HAVE DIFFICULTY

- Begin and end by spinning slowly. If difficulty persists, spin slowly throughout.
- If you have shoulder or neck problems with pain, let your arms bend at the elbows, rather than fully extending them to lessen the demand on the muscles in those areas.
- Do fewer repetitions until you feel more comfortable.
- If you have a problem with dizziness, pick three more focal points in addition to the first one. Using the image of the clock face, choose points at 12, 3, 6, and 9. Each point should offer something specific you can look at such as a window, a lamp, a piece of furniture, and a picture. Whenever you are facing those points, let your eyes focus on each object for the moment. Be sure your palms are facing down — this can help prevent dizziness, too.

  To regain equilibrium, when you finish spinning, stand with your feet shoulder-width apart. Touch the palms of your hands to your chest and look down at your thumbs. Hold this position until the dizziness subsides.

IF YOU WANT MORE CHALLENGE

- Spin faster, but never so fast that you lose your balance.

Spinning can cause nausea, headache, and a loss of balance. When you first begin doing this rite, spin slowly. Always go clockwise.

CHECK WITH YOUR DOCTOR
Because spinning might aggravate certain health conditions, seek professional advice if you have multiple sclerosis, Parkinson's or a Parkinson-like disease, Meniere's disease, vertigo, a seizure disorder, pregnancy with nausea, or are taking drugs that can cause dizziness. If you have an enlarged heart, a heart valve problem, or have suffered a heart attack within the past three months, do not do this rite without your doctor's explicit permission.

Rite Number Two

HELPS RELIEVE
* Arthritis
* Osteoporosis
* Irregular menses
* Symptoms of menopause
* Digestive and bowel problems
* Back pain
* Stiffness of the legs and neck

HEALTH BENEFITS
Rite Number Two has a restorative effect on the thyroid gland, the adrenals, the kidneys, the organs of the digestive system, and the sexual organs and glands, including the prostate and the uterus. It's helpful for irregular menstrual cycles and alleviating some of the symptoms of menopause. It has a posi-

tive impact on digestive and bowel problems. It's good for circulation and respiration, toning the heart muscles and the diaphragm, and the lymphatic flow. The movement also strengthens the abdomen, legs, and arms; releases tension from the lower back, which helps with pain; and has a beneficial effect on stiffness in the legs and neck. It can be of help to those suffering from arthritis of the hips and neck, and for those with osteoporosis in the legs, hips, pelvis and neck. It also speeds up the spin of chakras 5, 3, 2, and 1, in the throat, the upper and lower areas of the abdomen, and the tailbone.

Starting Position

- Lie flat on the floor, legs extended, face up. It's best to do this on a thick carpet, an exercise mat, or some sort of padded surface to cushion the spine and avoid contact with a cold floor.

- Place your arms close to your sides, parallel to your body, palms against the floor, fingers together.

Action

- Breathe in through your nose as you raise your head off the floor, tucking your chin against your chest. At the same time, lift both legs up together, bringing them as close to vertical as you can.

- It is important to keep your legs as straight as possible. If you are unable to keep your legs perfectly straight, let your knees bend only as much as is absolutely necessary. Work towards being able to raise your legs without bending your knees.

- Slowly lower your head and your legs back to the floor at the same time, still trying to keep your legs as straight as possible. Breathe out gently through your nose as you do this.

- Allow all your muscles to relax for a moment and then repeat this movement.

Rite Number Two

Tips

- As you lift your legs, press strongly down into the floor with palms, forearms, elbows, and shoulders.
- Keep your abdomen pulled in, and keep your mental focus on your abdomen. Your head should come up in a relaxed way and down slowly as your legs are lowered to the floor.

If You Have Difficulty

- Put a folded towel or blanket under your hips to get more momentum. When you notice that it has become easier for you to do this movement, stop using the towel.
- Increase the number of repetitions slowly and pause when necessary between repetitions.
- To help lift your legs, try a different way of breathing. Breathe in first when you are in the starting position. Then breathe out strongly as you raise your head and legs. Breathe in again when you've completed the upward movement and then breathe out slowly as you release your head and legs and bring them back down. When it becomes easier to lift your legs, shift to the breathing pattern described in the Action section for this rite.
- If you're unable to do this rite, substitute the warm-up called Abdominal Strengthener (see page 123).

If You Want More Challenge

- If you're able to lift your legs to a vertical position without bending your knees, then let them extend back over your upper body, toes pointing towards the floor.
- Do all your repetitions at a faster pace.

Precautions

Do this rite very slowly and increase the number of repetitions by one or two per week if you have ulcers, lower back pain, neck pain, high blood pressure that is being controlled with medication, weak abdominal muscles, excessive tension or stiffness in your shoulders or legs, multiple sclerosis, Parkinson's or a Parkinson-like disease, fibromyositis, or chronic fatigue syndrome. Menstruating women should be aware that it may aggravate cramping and interrupt or stop menstrual flow.

CHECK WITH YOUR DOCTOR

If you have a hiatal hernia, hernia, hyperthyroid condition, Meniere's disease, vertigo, or a seizure disorder, seek advice from your health care practitioner about whether this exercise is safe for you. If you are pregnant, have had abdominal surgery within six months, uncontrolled high blood pressure or hyperthyroidism, severe arthritis of the spine, or disc disease get your doctor's permission before doing this rite. If you have an enlarged heart, heart valve problem, or have suffered a heart attack within the past three months, do not do this rite without your doctor's explicit approval.

Rite Number Three

HELPS RELIEVE

- ◆ Arthritis
- ◆ Irregular or sluggish menses
- ◆ Symptoms of menopause
- ◆ Digestive problems
- ◆ Back and neck pain
- ◆ Sinus congestion

HEALTH BENEFITS

Like Rite Number Two, Rite Number Three rejuvenates the thyroid gland, the adrenals, kidneys, all digestive system organs, and the sexual organs and glands including the prostate and uterus. It's particularly good for menopausal women and menstruating women who tend to have irregular or sluggish periods. It tones and strengthens the abdomen, tones the diaphragm, deepens breathing, and releases muscle tension in the lower back and neck, alleviating pain and stiffness in those areas. It can help clear sinus congestion and relieve the symptoms of arthritis in the neck and upper back. Doing this movement speeds up the spin of all the chakras, especially 5, 3, and 2 in the throat and the upper and lower abdomen, increasing your general sense of vitality and energy.

Starting Position

- Kneel on the floor with your lower legs extended behind you, toes curled under, and the rest of your body erect.

- Grasp your thighs with your hands, thumbs facing forward, and breathe in through your nose.

Action

- Breathe out through your nose as you gently roll your head and neck forward, tucking your chin against your chest.

- Breathe in slowly and deeply as you lean backward, angling your torso over your lower legs. As your spine arches, your head follows, bending back gently as far as it can go.

- Breathe out and return to your starting position. Breathe in and repeat.

Rite Number Three

Tips

♦ For support and balance, brace your arms and hands against your thighs as you lean backward and come forward.

♦ Keep your head and neck relaxed.

If You Have Difficulty

♦ If you experience pain in your knees, put a folded towel or blanket under them.

♦ If you're unable to do this rite, do the warm-up called Thigh Strengthener instead (see page 136).

If You Want More Challenge

♦ Do all your repetitions at a faster pace.

Precautions

If you are taking medication for high blood pressure, do not allow your head to be positioned lower than your heart. If you have lower back or neck pain, weak abdominal muscles, recurring headaches, multiple sclerosis, Parkinson's or a Parkinson-like disease, fibromyositis, or chronic fatigue syndrome perform each repetition of this movement very slowly and add only one or two repetitions per week.

Check With Your Doctor

If you suffer from a hernia, hiatal hernia, uncontrolled high blood pressure, severe arthritis of the spine, disc disease, hyperthyroidism, Meniere's disease, vertigo, or a seizure disorder, check with your health care practitioner before doing this rite. Pregnant women and those who have had abdominal surgery within six months should seek advice from a doctor. If you have an enlarged heart, a heart valve problem, or have suffered a heart attack within the past three months, do not do this rite without your doctor's explicit approval.

Rite Number Four

HELPS RELIEVE

* Arthritis
* Osteoporosis
* Irregular or sluggish menses
* Symptoms of menopause
* Sinus congestion

HEALTH BENEFITS

Rite Number Four has an invigorating effect on the thyroid gland, the digestive system, the sexual organs and glands including the prostate and uterus, circulation, and lymphatic flow. It tones the abdomen, heart muscle and diaphragm, and strengthens the abdomen, thighs, arms, and shoulders. If you have sinus congestion, you may find that it helps clear your nasal passages. If you have arthritis in your neck, shoulders, hips, and knees, you may find this movement especially helpful to relieve symptoms. The same is true for people with osteoporosis in their arms, legs, and pelvis. It also deepens breathing and quickens the major chakras related to the areas of the throat, chest, upper and lower abdomen, and tailbone (chakras 5, 4, 3, 2, 1) and the minor chakra corresponding to the region of the knees, stimulating core energy and vitality and offering a special boost to the immune system. Sluggish or missed menstrual cycles and the symptoms of menopause can also be positively influenced by this movement.

Rite Number Four

Starting Position

♦ Sit on the floor, spine straight, legs fully extended in front of you, feet apart about the width of your shoulders.

♦ Place the palms of your hands down on the floor, alongside your buttocks, arms straight, fingers pointing toward your toes. Breathe in.

Action

♦ Breathe out and tuck your chin down against your chest. Breathe in again slowly as you let your head sink back as far as it will naturally

go. Raise your torso up as you continue this slow, deep inhalation. Your torso will be supported by your arms and lower legs. Your knees should be bent, positioned over your ankles, your arms straight, perpendicular to the floor. Your chest, abdomen, and upper legs should form a bridge or arch. Your feet should be flat on the floor.

- In this position, tense every muscle in your body and hold your breath. Then breathe out, gradually and thoroughly emptying your lungs as you relax every muscle and return to the original, starting position.

- Rest a moment, breathe in, then repeat.

TIPS

* Press your palms and heels strongly downward into the floor as you raise your torso.
* Thrust your pelvis upward, keeping your mental focus on this movement.
* Keep your buttocks squeezed together to protect your lower back.
* If you have symptoms of menopause, keep your abdomen pulled in.
* Pretend you're pressing a beach ball between your knees to keep them together, in line over your ankles.
* Keep your head in line with your spine. Begin with your head in a position so that your chin is touching your chest. Then go back to the normal head position, with your head parallel to the floor, but be sure not to move your head back past the parallel position.

IF YOU HAVE DIFFICULTY

* Practice thigh-strengthening and thigh-building exercises 3 times a day (see warm-up, page 136).
* Raise your torso up only as high as you can comfortably. Try pressing higher gradually, over time. Remember, there's no rush.
* If your wrists hurt or you have carpal tunnel syndrome, form your hands into fists to support your torso.
* If you are unable to do this rite, do the Bridge Warm-up instead (see page 120).

IF YOU WANT MORE CHALLENGE

* Do all your repetitions at a faster pace.

PRECAUTIONS

Do this rite slowly and add only one or two repetitions per week if you have high blood pressure that is being controlled with medication, ulcers, lower back pain, neck pain, weak abdominal muscles, weakness or stiffness in the shoulders or legs; multiple sclerosis, Parkinson's or a Parkinson-like disease, fibromyositis, carpal tunnel syndrome, or chronic fatigue syndrome. It may aggravate cramping or stop menstrual flow if done during menses.

CHECK WITH YOUR DOCTOR

If you are diagnosed with any of the following conditions, this rite should be done only with the approval of your health care practitioner: hernia, hiatal hernia, hyperthyroidism, Meniere's disease, vertigo, and a seizure disorder. If you are pregnant, have had abdominal surgery within six months, suffer from a severe hernia or hiatal hernia, uncontrolled high blood pressure, severe arthritis of the spine or disc disease, seek your doctor's advice before trying to do this rite. If you have an enlarged heart, heart valve problem, or have suffered a heart attack within the past three months, do not do this rite without your doctor's explicit approval.

Rite Number Five

HELPS RELIEVE

* Arthritis
* Osteoporosis
* Irregular or sluggish menses
* Sinus congestion
* Digestive and bowel problems
* Back pain
* Leg and neck stiffness

HEALTH BENEFITS

Rite Number Five rejuvenates the thyroid gland, adrenals, kidneys, all the organs of the digestive system, and the sexual organs and glands, including the prostate and uterus. It promotes improved circulation and lymphatic flow, which has a positive impact on the immune system, stimulates deeper breathing, energy, and vitality, and quickens all the chakras. It tones the abdomen, heart muscle, and diaphragm, strengthens the abdomen, legs, and arms, and helps with lower back pain as well as leg and neck stiffness. Like Rites Number Two, Three, and Four it is especially useful in alleviating the symptoms of menopause and irregular or sluggish menstrual periods. It also clears the sinuses, reduces digestive and bowel problems, helps those suffering from osteoporosis in the arms and legs, and may bring relief to those who suffer from arthritis of the hips, back, shoulders, hands, and feet.

Rite Number Five

Rite Number Five: Starting Position

- Begin by lying face down with your legs extended and your toes curled under. Your hands should be placed directly under your shoulders with your palms down. Your feet should be spaced apart more or less the width of your shoulders, in line with your hands, so as to give you a solid base.

- Lift your body, including your legs, by fully extending your arms perpendicular to the floor and flexing your toes. This position resembles a modified push-up; your spine should be arched, your chest raised, and your lower back in a sagging position.

Action

- Slowly breathe in through your nose as you gently move your head back as far as possible.

- Continue breathing in as you bend at the hips, bringing your body up into an inverted V. As you move into this position, your head will naturally come forward. Tuck your chin against your chest so you can see your feet, which are now almost flat on the floor with only your heels slightly raised.

- Breathe out, thoroughly emptying your lungs as you return to the arched position with your arms and legs straight. Breathe in and repeat.

TIPS

- Remember that you do not come back to the original starting position of lying flat on the floor until you've completed your full cycle of repetitions.
- Keep your abdomen pulled in and be sure to squeeze your buttocks to protect your lower back.
- Keep your mental focus on your shoulders, the backs of your legs, and the opening and releasing of your chest. Visualize lifting your buttocks and tailbone up towards the sky.
- Keep your head and neck relaxed to avoid neck strain.

IF YOU HAVE DIFFICULTY

- Keep your thighs on the floor and lift only your torso until your arms become stronger.
- Do wrist-, arm-, and shoulder-strengthening exercises 3 times a day (see warm-ups, pages 115-138).
- If you have wrist pain or carpal tunnel syndrome, instead of positioning your hands flat on the floor, make them into fists and put the pressure on your knuckles.
- If you experience knee pain, allow your knees to bend

slightly when you initially lift your torso and thighs off the floor.

- If you're unable to do Rite Number Five, do the Downward Dog warm-up in its place (see page 127).

If You Want More Challenge
- Do all your repetitions at a faster pace.

Precautions
Do this movement slowly and, if necessary, add only one or two repetitions per week if you have ulcers, lower back pain, neck pain, weak abdominal muscles, shoulder or leg stiffness or weakness, multiple sclerosis, Parkinson's or a Parkinson-like disease, fibromyositis, carpal tunnel syndrome, or chronic fatigue syndrome.

Check with Your Doctor
Seek your doctor's advice before doing this rite if you have high blood pressure, a hiatal hernia, a hernia, severe arthritis of the spine, disc disease, hyperthyroidism, Meniere's disease, vertigo, a seizure disorder, if you're pregnant, or have had abdominal surgery within six months. If you have an enlarged heart, a heart valve problem, or have suffered a heart attack within the past three months, do not do this rite without your doctor's explicit approval.

After the Five Rites: Relaxation

It's useful to spend 5 to 10 minutes relaxing after completing all five of the rites. Try the following technique: Lie flat on the floor, on your back, with your eyes closed. Do the Body Scan with Abdominal Breathing described in the warm-up section of this chapter. This relaxation period, characterized by deep, slow, easy breathing, releases any tension that may have built up as you exercised, reduces the possibility of any residual stiffness, and maximizes the benefits that have accrued to all the nerves, glands, and organs of your body. It gives the chakras time to balance their energy and gives the mind an opportunity to come into a calm state that can influence the rest of your day.

Rite Number Six

The sixth rite is in a category of its own. In *Ancient Secret of the Fountain of Youth, Book 1,* it is discussed separately from the other five.

Rite Number Six involves sexual abstention as the ultimate method for achieving a remarkably youthful appearance. The explanation is that the life force energy which normally expresses itself in sexuality is redirected into the other energy centers of the body. Colonel Bradford distinguishes between the Western monastic tradition, which has concentrated on suppressing such impulses, and the Eastern view that sexual energy can be channeled in other directions and transformed for higher purposes. (See Chapter Four for a more detailed discussion of Rite Number Six.)

Celibacy is not an uncommon demand for those on a spiritual path. In yoga, sexual abstention has often been practiced in order to conserve energy. Some view the "rerouting" of sexual impulses as a way to enhance spiritual development. It is a choice that takes one out of the ordinary flow of human life, and it is one way to shift the focus of daily living from the secular to the spiritual.

Although the Colonel reports that he was told that complete abstention was necessary in order to practice the sixth rite, I'm not so sure myself. Sexual abstinence is not a requirement in all Tibetan Buddhist sects. My own training leads me to believe that the idea behind Rite Number Six can be adapted, and the rite can be used to help find creative new ways for the expression of sexual energy, even if a person does not lead a completely chaste life.

Most people, on occasion, have an excess of sexual energy or experience sexual feelings when there is no partner to share them with. This energy can manifest itself as nervousness and anxiety, and might be expressed as overeating or constant fidgeting. The practice of the sixth rite provides a very healthy, balancing outlet for helping to get rid of this tension. The result is that after doing the exercise, you are more relaxed, and that, of course, as I've said earlier, is deeply rejuvenating.

I believe we can use sexual energy to fuel other areas of our lives, and other pursuits. Rite Number Six works to move this energy so that it's actually available for this purpose. So even if you are not interested in being completely celibate, I think the sixth rite has a value. It should be done only when you feel a sexual urge that, for whatever reasons, will go ungratified, or you have an excess of sexual energy.

Rite Number Six

Starting Position

- Stand up straight, feet slightly apart, planted firmly on the floor, arms at your sides.

Action

- Slowly breathe out as you bend over from the waist, placing your hands on your knees. Continue breathing out until you've forced out all the air in your lungs.

- With your lungs empty, return to an upright posture. Place your hands on your hips and press down, which will push your shoulders up. The key to the power of this movement is that as your shoulders are pushed up, you must pull in your abdomen and raise your chest

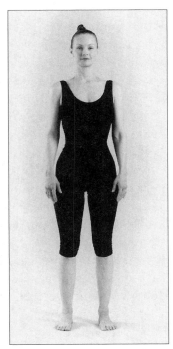

as much as possible. And you must do this without breathing in. This is what moves the energy into other centers. Hold this position as long as you can.

- When you must take a breath, let the air flow in through your nose. When your lungs feel full, breathe out through your mouth. As you breathe out, let your abdomen out, your shoulders relax, and your arms drop from your hips to hang naturally at your sides.

- Take several deep breaths, breathing in and out through your nose. This marks the completion of one full repetition of this rite. It should be done only 2 or 3 times.

A Few Final Suggestions

- Practice the rites in sequence, from Rite Number One to Rite Number Five.
- Do the Five Rites every day. Of course, there will be days when it's just impossible to take the 20 or 30 minutes necessary to do the whole routine. But don't make a habit of skipping them for more than a day now and then, or you'll never have a chance to discover the benefits the rites can bring to your life and health.
- If you are sick, busy, or stressed, it's much better to do each rite only 3 times than to skip doing them completely. It takes less than five minutes to do the rites 3 times each. Think of it as washing your face instead of taking a shower. No matter how rushed you are in the morning, there's always enough time to wash your face.
- If you do skip more than a day, I advise taking a few steps back in your routine. Do fewer repetitions than you were doing and build yourself back up again over the course of a week. Never try to add extra repetitions to make up for those you missed. I can't overemphasize the fact that, whether you are resuming the routine after a lapse or just beginning, it's important to gradually work your way up to the full 21 repetitions of each rite.
- Even if you are physically able to do all 21 repetitions from the start, follow the instructions as they've been given. Build up incrementally to the full cycle. Unlike calisthenics or other common forms of exercise, the rites deal with more subtle things than simple muscle strength and agility. Respect the process. Strive for quality rather than quantity.
- Consistent practice according to the instructions insures your success. If you do this, you're more likely not to get discouraged and you'll find it's not hard to stick with your daily commitment. You'll be less likely to strain yourself or expe-

rience uncomfortable reactions such as nausea or dizziness.

- Twenty-one repetitions of each rite are all that's needed. There's simply no reason to do more. If you wish, you can do the rites twice a day, upon awakening and in the evening at least two hours after eating. Or you may want to use one of those sessions for other, complementary modes of relaxation and self-exploration, like yoga.

- It's best to do the rites first thing in the morning on an empty stomach. I recommend getting up a half-hour earlier to give yourself enough time to do the rites in an unhurried way. I know that can be hard, especially at first, but it's well worth the effort. You'll start your day feeling wide awake, relaxed, and energetic, often finding that you require less sleep.

- It's important to wear loose, comfortable clothing that does not restrict your movements. Sweats, shorts and a T-shirt, pajamas, or even your underwear are ideal. I think it's best to have bare feet, but if your feet are cold, wearing socks is fine. As with any other form of exercise, those who wear eye glasses should remove them.

- The rites are meant to help you relax, so it's important not to surround the practice of them with a great deal of agitation and conflict. Choose the most comfortable, quiet, reasonably private place you can, with enough room for you to stretch out fully.

- If the floor is not carpeted you might want to have an exercise or yoga mat, a piece of thin foam, or a thick, plush carpet remnant to lie on. Approach the exercises with a focused state of mind. This is a time to pay attention to your body, to learn to listen to it. Although I know that some people feel differently, I think it's best not to have any type of music playing in the background. It becomes something else to distract the mind from the body.

- A quiet atmosphere for doing the rites is ideal but perhaps, in your life, that may not always be possible. Accept that, don't fight it, and don't let oversleeping or the commotion of your household become an excuse not to do your practice.

- As you do the rites, try not to think about your day, your obligations, and your concerns. When you notice that you are preoccupied and have drifted away from an awareness of the sensations in your body, bring the focus of your attention back to the movements you are doing. If you're anything like me, you'll have to keep doing this again and again. Concentrating on your breathing can help you focus and it will help you relax.

- The Five Rites can fit into your life. Unlike many techniques and schools of thought that have come to us from the East, doing the rites does not require you to change your lifestyle, your world view, or your religion. Despite the fact that they are rooted in an ancient spiritual discipline, they can be done strictly as a form of exercise.

- The rites are good preparation and support for those who are interested in meditation. It's advisable to do them first, and then meditate. Even if you don't meditate, you might want to try taking time afterwards to sit still, relax, and clear your mind. Just lie on your back quietly for 10 or 15 minutes after completing the routine. Because relaxation plays a critical role in the body's ability to heal and nourish itself, this can only further accentuate the benefits of the rites.

My Own Experience

I've developed my own morning routine that gives me all the benefits of a full workout plus a cup of coffee without having to use any special equipment, commit so much time, or suffer the harmful effects of caffeine.

I do all the warm-up exercises right after I wake up. They help me focus my attention in my body and dispel that groggy, tired feeling I often have upon awakening. I think of it as getting my engine started. Then I do the Five Rites. Their effect is rapid and clear. I have a sense of heightened mental clarity, and experience a surge of both physical and emotional strength. I get a real sense of accomplishment and self-satisfaction. And the rites have helped me with the yoga postures that I also do. I always follow this with a very satisfying period of relaxation or formal meditation.

My days are very full. They start early and often end late. When I do the Five Rites, I feel ready to face my life and all its demands, knowing I'll have the good health and energy I need.

I wish you well as you embark on your own practice of the Five rites, confident that you're on the road to real, long-lasting health and vitality.

Jeff Migdow, M.D., received his medical education at the University of Illinois in Chicago, and did his internship at George Washington University Hospital in Washington, D.C. He has been in general practice, with a special focus on holistic medicine, for 15 years. While a college student, Dr. Migdow read about the health benefits of yoga and took up the practice himself. His medical studies revealed a definite correspondence between Western scientific fact and the basic principles of yoga, making it clear that yoga's beneficial effects on the body could be explained biologically. And he noticed that the exercises did indeed have a positive impact on his own health and stamina.

As an intern, he was regularly on call seven days a week, often staying up all night two or three times a week. With little time to devote to a long and complicated yoga routine, he created his own short series of yoga postures, exercises he could do in just ten minutes. Dr. Migdow is certain that these helped him get through this very difficult and stressful period. And unlike many of his colleagues at that time, he felt healthy and energetic.

Yoga continued to be an important part of Migdow's life after he went into private practice. He was especially interested in Hatha yoga, the form that emphasizes physical exercises. Several years ago, a patient told him about the Five Rites and gave him a copy of Ancient Secret of the Fountain of Youth. Dr. Migdow was immediately attracted to the rites because they reminded him of yoga postures but required less time. Not only did he begin to do them himself, but he also began to recommend them to his patients. Many reported to him that after doing the rites for only two or three months, they felt healthier, more motivated, and energized, and Dr. Migdow noticed that the rites, like the practice of yoga, seemed to speed up the healing process.

Currently, Dr. Migdow is on the staff of The Kripalu Center in Lenox, Massachusetts, one of the largest yoga-oriented health care facilities in the world. He continues to recommend both the practice of yoga and the Five Rites because he is convinced that they offer health and healing benefits, representing a way that people can actively help themselves feel better and live more fully.

Laura Faye Taxel has been a writer, journalist, and researcher for more than 20 years. Her work has appeared in numerous national and local publications including Ladies Home Journal, Parenting, Natural Health, New Age, The Cleveland Plain Dealer Sunday Magazine, The Akron Beacon Journal Sunday Magazine and Cleveland Parent.

Laura is the author of Cleveland Ethnic Eats (Gray and Company, Inc., 1995), and she is currently working on several book projects on a variety of topics including health and education.

CHAPTER SIX

Food Combining
and Other Dietary Advice

by Dr. Stanley S. Bass and Chet Day

In discussing various subjects related to health, longevity, and the Five Rites, Colonel Bradford offers advice on diet, nutrition, and the important role of food in human life. As Bradford explains, proper diet contributes to "wonderful signs of physical improvement." Let's review some of the specific dietary recommendations he offers.

The key to good health, according to the Colonel, lies with a time-proven method of eating simple foods. According to Bradford, hard-working Tibetan lamas produced their own food and ate a predominantly vegetarian diet with the addition of some eggs, butter, and cheese.

In addition, the lamas ate only one kind of food at a time. While you don't need to go to that extreme, explains Colonel Bradford, "I would recommend that you keep starches, fruits, and vegetables separate from meats, fish, and fowl at your meals."

The Colonel also warns against a common problem many of us face—overeating! After living in the monastery for two years, says Bradford, "One of the first things I noticed when I arrived in one of the major cities of India was the large amount of food consumed by everyone who could afford to do so. I saw one man eat in just one meal a quantity of food sufficient to feed and completely nourish four hard-working lamas."

Moreover, Colonel Bradford found the conglomeration of foods eaten in the same meal appalling. "Having been in the habit of eating one or two foods at a meal," he said, "I was amazed to count 23 varieties of food one evening at my host's table. No wonder Westerners have such miserable health. They seem to know little or nothing about the relationship of diet to health and strength."

In a final piece of excellent advice, Colonel Bradford tells us to thoroughly chew our food and eat slowly. "Mastication is the first important step in breaking food down so that it can be assimilated by the body," he explains. "Everything one eats should be digested in the mouth before it is digested in the stomach."

The Colonel summarizes the benefits of proper eating and food combining this way: "The right combinations of food, the right amounts of food, and the right method of eating combine to produce wonderful results. If you are overweight, it will help you reduce. And if you are underweight, it will help you gain."

And then he gives five rules for building better health through proper eating:

1. Never eat starch and meat at the same meal, though if you are strong and healthy it need not cause you too much concern now.

2. If coffee bothers you, drink it black, using no milk or cream. If it still bothers you, eliminate it from your diet.

3. Chew your food to a liquid, and cut down on the amount of food you eat.

4. Eat raw egg yolks once a day, every day. Take them either just before or after meals — not during meals.[2]

5. Reduce the variety of foods you eat in one meal to a minimum.

In this chapter, we will expand upon Colonel Bradford's dietary recommendations.

Natural Hygiene and the Fountain of Youth

Although it may be compatible with Tibetan dietary practices, Peter Kelder probably derived the bulk of Colonel Bradford's dietary advice from a school of health-building popular in the 1930s (and today, as well) called Natural Hygiene.

For the most part, a modern Natural Hygiene point of view would applaud Colonel Bradford's rules. A hygienist would, however, recommend completely eliminating coffee from the diet and would also warn against the use of raw eggs because of possible salmonella contamination.

Peter Kelder probably read and heard about the principles of Natural Hygiene through the work of Dr. Herbert M. Shelton, the man who almost single-handedly resurrected the nineteenth century school of thought, originally known simply as "Hygiene". Dr. Shelton consolidated, refined, and updated the principles of Hygiene and gave it the new name, Natural Hygiene. Besides publishing a monthly magazine and a seven-volume tutorial on the subject, Dr. Shelton also wrote for Bernarr MacFadden's *Physical Culture* magazines, as well as for the other popular alternative health publications of the time. For years Natural Hygiene had a small but dedicated following. Then, in 1985, Harvey and Marilyn Diamond published *Fit for Life*, a health and diet book that explained the principles of Natural Hygiene. With its simple prose and anecdotal stories of

---

2. Public health authorities now warn against eating raw eggs, due to possible contamination from salmonella bacteria, which can cause food poisoning.

success, *Fit for Life* soon became a bestseller. It taught many people how to eat and live more sensibly, and it popularized the ideas of Natural Hygiene.

Today, thousands of people belong to the American Natural Hygiene Society. Although hundreds of books have been written about Natural Hygiene, at its heart you will find a few simple rules of living. If you practice these simple, common sense rules, your life and health will undergo improvements you can't even imagine:

1. Eat simple, predominantly uncooked vegetarian foods.
2. Combine your foods sensibly. (Read on for a discussion of food combining.)
3. Breathe fresh air.
4. Get moderate sunlight on as much of your body as possible each day. Never let yourself burn, however.
5. Drink pure water as thirst demands.
6. Rest and sleep at least eight hours a day.
7. Exercise your body for at least 20 minutes, three times a week. Some authorities recommend aerobic exercise such as jogging, swimming, biking, and so on; others recommend weight-lifting or "quick burst" movement. Most agree that brisk walking for 30 minutes every other day is a great all-around exercise.
8. Keep your body clean.
9. Maintain emotional poise at all times through acting, rather than reacting.
10. Avoid extremes of temperature.
11. Spend time with nurturing family and friends.

Of course, not everyone wants to eat a vegetarian, predominantly raw food diet as encouraged by Natural Hygiene. Recognizing this, Dr. Shelton developed and refined specific rules for properly combining a variety of foods for optimal digestion. When foods are properly combined, digestion works most efficiently, nutrients are easily absorbed, and overall health improves.

What Is Food Combining?

Food combining refers to the mixing of different foods at the moment of eating—such as taking a forkful of tossed salad, then a steamed vegetable, then a mouthful of grain or bread, followed by a bite of meat, then a sip of fruit juice or beverage, and then back to the salad. Most people repeat this cycle of constant alternation until they've cleaned their plate. Then they complete the meal with one or two desserts and maybe a beverage.

Mixing these various foods causes a problem because each type of food takes a different amount of time to digest. (See digestion times of common foods on pages 182-185.) The most concentrated food, usually a protein, takes the longest amount of time to digest, and it is the first type of food to be worked on by the stomach. The digestion of protein takes hours. If fat is present beyond a very small amount, digestion takes even longer.

Quick-digesting foods, like fruits and vegetables, must linger in the stomach, trapped, waiting for the most concentrated foods to be digested first. This process can take up to eight hours. While waiting, the fruit, cooked and raw vegetables, and certain starches undergo some decomposition and fermentation. As the stomach struggles to digest this mess, it produces gas, acid, and even alcohol, not to mention indigestion. Complete digestion must wait until the food reaches the intestines, where additional enzymes are needed to break down the undigested foods, and minerals neutralize the acids. Put simply, the principles of food combining provide guidelines for the foods you should and should not consume together for optimal digestion and good health.

Health Problems from Improper Food Combining

What problems come with improper food combining? The specific answer depends on the individual of course, but in general those who don't combine their foods compatibly will suffer the ill effects of food fermentation in the stomach and experience, at a minimum, indigestion and/or heartburn after meals. Other problems include gas, belching, hyperacidity, bloating, sour stomach, fluid retention, and mental dullness with an inability to concentrate for hours after eating.

With improper food combining, digestion can be delayed for two to eight hours. Too much energy is needed for the digestive process, creating fatigue and the need for extra sleep and rest. This can cause hypersensitivity, irritability, depression, negativity, cynicism, and an accumulation of toxins in the bloodstream and body.

Additionally, the accumulation of toxins from indigestion leads to colds and lays the groundwork for many ailments and diseases, weakens the immune system, causes premature aging, loss of sexual drive and ability, and can weaken sperm and ovum cells. In short, improper food combining can cause the deterioration of physical, mental, and emotional health, shortening your life span.

The Rewards of Proper Food Combining

Those who practice correct food combining notice an immediate improvement in their health because the load on the digestive organs has been lessened. Proper food combining ensures better nutrition, better digestion, more comfort, less distress, and less gas. Because the body produces fewer fermented and toxic substances many people see problems with food allergies disappear. Individuals who have suffered volcanic gas for years often find complete relief within a few days once they start properly combining their foods. Perhaps best of all, correct food combining produces increased energy and promotes weight loss.

Here's a summary of the health benefits you'll enjoy as a result of proper food combining:

1. *Improved Digestion* – If you follow the rules for food combining beginning on page 185 your digestion should improve significantly. In a matter of days, the gas, sour stomach, heartburn, and constipation that has plagued you for years will improve or disappear entirely. Often, people say, "I can't follow food combining. It's too hard." We tell such people to try it for one week as an experiment. We make this suggestion because we know once they enjoy the improved digestion that comes with food combining they won't want to go back to the old way of eating.

2. *Weight Loss* – When you eat properly combined foods, you'll start looking forward to those morning trips to the bathroom scale. Why? Because the excess pounds, hip-hugging fat, jiggly arm flesh, and puckered cellulite will burn away like crazy! Most people who practice good combining really appreciate the way three to five pounds of real fat and not just water loss falls away from their bodies week after week after week. I (Day) personally went from a gross 192 pounds on my 5'7" frame to a comfortable 145 pounds the first four months after I started combining my foods and living the principles of Natural Hygiene!

   Because of better digestion, your body won't require so much water to flush out the cells and won't be bloated from fluid retention; you'll be trimmer and slimmer. Since you'll be satisfied with less food when you combine properly, your daily calorie intake will go down and so will your body weight! Your appetite will be satisfied with less food because you'll absorb and be able to use more nutrients.

Additionally, you'll save money because your hunger will be satisfied with less food. And, more important, the less you eat, the longer you'll live. There'll be less wear and tear from digestion. Luigi Cornaro, a fourteenth century Italian nobleman and writer, lived to be 102 years old on two meals a day totaling 12 ounces of food and 14 ounces of grape juice because he combined his food properly and saved his digestive energy. He began this when he was 35 years old and his health was rapidly declining from a life of overindulgence. His doctors told him to live more sensibly or he would die. He took their advice and became one of the great health writers of all time.

3. *Energy Gain* – When you combine your foods properly, your body doesn't need as much energy for digestion. As a result, you'll probably feel a noticeable increase in your energy level.

4. *Overall Good Health* – You'll awaken feeling more refreshed from digestive rest as a result of proper combining. You'll feel better and more alert and will need less sleep. You'll be more cheerful in disposition because you'll avoid the internal warfare of foods which do not combine well with each other. This will radiate to the consciousness as well-being and happiness.

Food Classifications for Proper Food Combining

The following classifications will help guide you as you learn to properly combine your foods and plan healthful meals. See "Digestion Times for Common Foods" for additional foods in each category.

PROTEINS

nuts and seeds	peanuts	eggs	soybeans
dried beans	dried peas	milk*	cheese
lentils	sunflower sprouts	garbanzo bean sprouts	
lentil sprouts	flesh foods (fish, poultry, meat)		

STARCHES

potatoes	sweet potatoes	fresh lima beans	globe artichokes
chestnuts	yams	winter squash	pumpkins
bread	pasta	cereals and grains	parsnips
coconuts	legumes	salsify ("vegetable oyster")	
mature, starchy corn			

FATS

avocados	vegetable oils	butter*	cream*	margarine	lard
olives	seeds	nuts	peanuts	soybeans	

ACID FRUITS	SUB-ACID FRUITS	SWEET FRUITS	MELON
orange	mango	banana	watermelon
grapefruit	cherry	date	honeydew
pineapple	apple	persimmon	muskmelon
strawberry	peach	sapote	cantaloupe
kiwi	plum	fresh fig	casaba
tomato	apricot	Thompson grapes	crenshaw
kumquat	berries	Muscat grapes	Christmas melon
lemon	most grapes	papaya	Persian melon
lime	pear	dried fruits	canary melon
pomegranate	nectarine		

LOW–STARCH AND NON–STARCHY VEGETABLES

celery	Brussels sprouts	cabbage	fresh, sweet corn
Chinese cabbage	cucumber	fresh, sweet peas	broccoli
cauliflower	summer squash	collards	bok choy
kohlrabi	sweet pepper	kale	turnips
eggplant	asparagus	carrots	alfalfa sprouts
onions	beets	spinach	lettuce
green beans	garlic		

*NOTE: Dairy products are not recommended.

Digestion Times for Common Foods

Use these guidelines for determining the digestion times of various foods, the best food combinations, and the maximum suggested amounts of each food to eat:

Water: When your stomach is empty, water leaves immediately and goes into the intestines.

Juices: *Fruit juice, vegetable juice, and vegetable broth* take 15 to 20 minutes to digest.

Semi-liquids: *Blended salads* (mix lettuce, tomato, celery, and cucumber in your blender until the moment the whirlpool starts, then eat much like soup), *blended vegetables*, or *blended fruits* take 20 to 30 minutes to digest.

Fruits: *Watermelon* takes 20 minutes to digest. It is best eaten as the only fruit in a meal. Have ⅛ to ¼ of a watermelon maximum. *Other melons (such as cantaloupe, crenshaw, honeydew)* take 30 minutes to digest. Two varieties may be combined occasionally, but eat no more than 16 ounces maximum at a meal.
Oranges, grapefruit, and grapes take 30 minutes to digest. Two varieties may be combined occasionally, but eat no more than 16 ounces maximum at a meal.
Apples, pears, peaches, cherries, and other sub-acid fruits take 40 minutes to digest. Two to three varieties may be eaten at a meal, but stay with a 12 to 16 ounce maximum.

Raw Vegetables: *Raw salad vegetables, such as tomato, lettuce (romaine, Boston, Bibb, red, leafy, garden,) cucumber, celery, red or green pepper, and other succulent vegetables* take 30 to 40 minutes to digest. If oil is added, digestion time increases to 60-plus minutes. Since all these vegetables digest in the same amount of time, they may be combined. You can blend them together, if you wish (see semi-liquids).

Steamed or Cooked Vegetables: *Leafy vegetables (such as escarole, spinach, kale, collards)* take 40 minutes to digest.
Zucchini, broccoli, cauliflower, string beans, yellow squash, and corn on the cob take 45 minutes to digest.
Root vegetables such as carrots, beets, parsnips, turnips take 50 minutes to digest.
Note: Two to three varieties of vegetables may be eaten together, 4 ounces each maximum, 8 ounces total. Eat the leafy vegetables first, the roots last.

Starchy Vegetables: *Jerusalem artichokes and leafy, acorn and butternut squashes, potatoes, sweet potatoes, yams, and chestnuts* require 60 minutes to digest. For a main dish, you may have two varieties, with a total of 16 ounces maximum.

Starches: *Brown rice, millet, buckwheat* (these three are preferred), *cornmeal, oats, quinoa, teff,* and *barley* take 60 to 90 minus to digest. Maximum amount is 4 ounces dry weight, which yields 13 ounces cooked weight.

Legumes—Starches and Protein: *Lentils, lima beans, chick peas, pigeon peas, kidney beans,* and so on require 90 minutes to digest. Maximum amount is 4 ounces dry weight, which yields 8 ounces cooked weight. One ounce to 1½ ounce dry weight may be cooked with 3 to 4 ounces rice, or eaten after rice. Soy beans take 120 minutes to digest. Eat a maximum of 1 to 4 ounces.

Seeds and Nuts: *Seeds, such as sunflower, pumpkin, pepita, and sesame,* take approximately 2 hours to digest. You can eat one or two varieties with a maximum amount of 1 to 4 ounces. *Nuts, such as almonds, filberts, peanuts (raw), cashews, Brazil, walnuts, and pecans,* take 2½ to 3 hours to digest. Eat only one type per meal with 3 ounces maximum, unless you do lots of heavy physical work. (Soaking seeds or nuts overnight and then grinding them just before eating speeds up digestion and assimilation.)

Dairy (not recommended): *Low-fat cottage cheese, low-fat pot cheese, and ricotta cheese* take approximately 90 minutes to digest. Eat a maximum of 4 to 8 ounces.

Whole milk cottage cheese takes 2 hours to digest. Eat a maximum of 4 to 8 ounces.
Whole milk hard cheese, such as Swiss and Muenster, takes 4 to 5 hours to digest. Eat a maximum of 2 to 4 ounces.
Note: Hard cheese requires a longer digestion time than most other foods because of the high concentration of fat and protein.

Animal Proteins: *Egg yolk* takes 30 minutes to digest; whole egg, 45 minutes. One to 2 maximum per day.
Fish such as cod, scrod, flounder, and filet of sole takes 30 minutes to digest. Eat a maximum of 4 to 6 ounces.
Salmon, trout, tuna, herring (more fatty fish) take 45 to 60 minutes to digest. Eat a maximum of 4 to 6 ounces. You may mix two varieties.
Chicken (without skin) takes 1½ to 2 hours to digest. Eat a maximum of 4 ounces.
Turkey (without skin) takes 2 to 2¼ hours to digest. Eat a maximum of 4 ounces.
Beef and lamb take 3 to 4 hours to digest. Eat a maximum of 4 ounces.
Pork takes 4½ to 5 hours to digest. Eat a maximum of 4 ounces.

Oils, Butter, Fat: *Olive oil or any cold-pressed oil* may be added to salad, steamed vegetables, or other foods. The same applies to butter, salted or unsalted (preferred), although dairy products are not recommended. Use a maximum of ½ to 1 ounce oil or 1 to 2 tablespoons butter.

The Nine Rules of Natural Hygiene Food Combining

Now that you have the food classifications and digestion times handy, let's look at Dr. Herbert Shelton's rules of food combining:

1. *Do not eat a concentrated protein and a concentrated starch at the same meal.* Colonel Bradford and the lamas stressed the singular importance of this food combining principle. Why? Protein can only be properly digested when the stomach produces a large amount of acid. However, acids destroy salivary amylase, the enzyme needed for the proper digestion of starch. Therefore, protein and starch cannot be properly digested at the same time. Does this mean no more "meat and potato" meals? Yes, if you want painless digestion and better health!

2. *Do not eat starchy foods and acid foods at the same meal.* (See explanation for #1.)

3. *Do not eat two concentrated proteins at the same meal.* Different types of protein require different digestion times and different modifications of the digestive secretions. Because the body works very hard to digest even one protein, digesting more than one would force the body to work too hard and would sap too much energy. By consuming only one type of protein per meal, you save digestive energy and avoid unnecessary fatigue.

4. *Do not eat acid fruits with proteins.* The enzyme pepsin, which is necessary for protein digestion, is destroyed by most acids, including fruit acids. Pepsin only remains active in the presence of hydrochloric acid.

5. *Do not eat fats with proteins.* Fats inhibit the flow of gastric juices and interfere with protein digestion.

6. *Do not eat starches and sugars together.* When you combine starch with sugar, the body begins to digest the sugar first. Sugar ferments in the stomach, creating acid which destroys the enzyme salivary amylase, needed for the digestion of starch. If you suffer from indigestion from eating fruits and cereal at breakfast, you now know the reason and how to prevent the problem. Eat the fruits by themselves and let the body digest the natural sugars to prevent the fermentation that is caused by mixing sugars with starches.

7. *Do not eat proteins and sugars together.* Sugars also interfere with protein digestion by inhibiting the secretion of gastric juice. Fermentation results because the sugars are digested after the proteins, and in the meantime must linger in the stomach waiting for the proteins to be digested.

8. *Do not eat melons with any other foods.* The body digests melons very quickly. Eat them at the beginning of a meal or by themselves so they can move lickety-split through the digestive tract. For most of my life I avoided watermelon and cantaloupe because they gave me terrible stomach cramps and gas. I now eat one type of melon at a sitting and relish the sweet, fresh taste and effortless digestion!

9. *Avoid milk and milk products, but if you must have them, do not combine them with any other foods.* Only infants have sufficient quantities of the milk-digesting enzyme rennin. Hygienists, as well as many medical doctors (including Dr. Spock, much to the dairy industry's chagrin), encourage people to eliminate milk and milk products from their diet. The absence of amylase enzymes in adults makes milk indigestible, thus producing many allergic reactions. In addition, milk should not

be combined with any other foods because of its high protein and fat content.

The rules of food combining may seem complicated to you at first. The chart on the following page will simplify them and help you plan meals.

How Colonel Bradford's Advice Stacks Up

As you can see from examining the rules of food combining, the lamas gave Colonel Bradford sound advice — advice which closely parallels the time-proven teachings of Natural Hygiene. In a few specific instances, however, Colonel Bradford's suggestions do warrant a second look.

For example, the Colonel states, "It is all right to make a meal of just meat. In fact, if you wish, you could have several kinds of meat in one meal. And it is all right to eat butter, eggs, and cheese with a meat meal, or dark bread and, in moderation, coffee or tea. But you must not end with anything sweet or starchy — no pies, cakes, or puddings."

Obviously, a Natural Hygienist would encourage you to *never* make a meal of just meat, since Hygienists (and modern medical research proves the case as well) know that the protein overload found in most meat meals often leads to problems. Additionally, having bread with a protein can in some people cause fermentation, gas, and stomach distress. Colonel Bradford's earlier advice to eat but a single food at a meal rings the bell of truth much louder than what he says in the paragraph you just read. Evidently, he allows this as a compromise in a transition diet to help people get started.

Colonel Bradford allows for milk, tea, and coffee drinking. This is also allowed as a compromise for beginners. Natural Hygiene tells us that our health improves for the better when

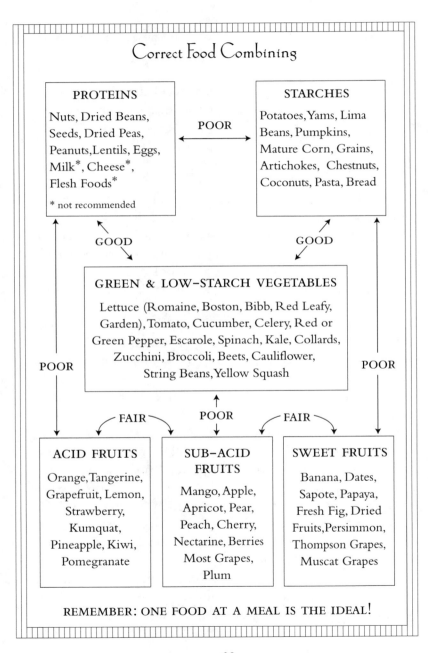

Correct Food Combining

PROTEINS

Nuts, Dried Beans, Seeds, Dried Peas, Peanuts, Lentils, Eggs, Milk*, Cheese*, Flesh Foods*

* not recommended

STARCHES

Potatoes, Yams, Lima Beans, Pumpkins, Mature Corn, Grains, Artichokes, Chestnuts, Coconuts, Pasta, Bread

POOR

GOOD   GOOD

GREEN & LOW-STARCH VEGETABLES

Lettuce (Romaine, Boston, Bibb, Red Leafy, Garden), Tomato, Cucumber, Celery, Red or Green Pepper, Escarole, Spinach, Kale, Collards, Zucchini, Broccoli, Beets, Cauliflower, String Beans, Yellow Squash

POOR   POOR

FAIR   POOR   FAIR

ACID FRUITS

Orange, Tangerine, Grapefruit, Lemon, Strawberry, Kumquat, Pineapple, Kiwi, Pomegranate

SUB-ACID FRUITS

Mango, Apple, Apricot, Pear, Peach, Cherry, Nectarine, Berries Most Grapes, Plum

SWEET FRUITS

Banana, Dates, Sapote, Papaya, Fresh Fig, Dried Fruits, Persimmon, Thompson Grapes, Muscat Grapes

REMEMBER: ONE FOOD AT A MEAL IS THE IDEAL!

you remove these substances from your diet. Tea and coffee contain alkaloids that harm human tissue, and pasteurized milk contains a protein component called casein, the same substance used to make one of the strongest wood glues known. Ever wonder why eating cheese or a lot of ice cream binds you up the next day and sends you lumbering for a laxative? Well, now you know.

Sorry, but contrary to what the dairy industry's high-priced ad campaigns would have you believe, milk does *not* do a body good. If you don't believe me, explain why my long-standing hemorrhoids disappeared when I stopped eating and drinking milk products (this on the advice of a colon surgeon). And if you don't put any credence in anecdotal evidence, please visit a library and read the medical research of the past 20 years which proves unequivocally that none of us should drink milk at all!

Although the Colonel doesn't say much about drinking beverages with meals (other than coffee or tea), the average person in our culture consumes a beverage with each meal. Natural Hygiene encourages you not to drink anything while eating because liquids dilute the enzymes and stomach acids that are working to digest the food. By drinking beverages while eating, you inhibit complete digestion! Some modern research argues against this conclusion, but those individuals who practice the "no drinking with meals" rule find that it works beautifully for them. Rather than relying on research, rely on yourself and experiment on your own body to find what works best for you.

Colonel Bradford praises raw eggs and we consider egg yolk the best protein available. But today's supermarket eggs all too often carry salmonella bacteria, so we don't recommend eating raw egg yolks. For soft-boiled eggs, bring the water to a boil and then shut off the heat. Keep the whole eggs in water for three minutes, then remove, and eat only the yolks. Discard the whites unless you are an athlete or doing physical labor.

Some claim that eating egg yolks promotes optimal brain functioning as well as physical well-being. Colonel Bradford would undoubtedly agree. Let's review what he said: "I had always known that egg yolks are nutritious, but I learned of their true value only after talking with another Westerner at the monastery, a man who had a background in biochemistry. He told me that common hen eggs contain fully half of the elements required by the brain, nerves, and organs of the body. It is true that these elements are needed only in small quantities, but they must be included in the diet if you are to be exceptionally robust and healthy, both mentally and physically."

And Colonel Bradford gives us more excellent advice when he tells us to thoroughly masticate our food. Hygiene teaches us to chew all food almost to a liquid before swallowing. Abbé Spallanzani (1729-1799), one of the pioneer observers of gastric digestion, found that cherries and grapes, when swallowed whole, even if entirely ripe, usually passed unbroken in the stools. This significant observation indicates the tremendous importance of thorough mastication of all food before swallowing. You can assimilate only those foods that are most liquefied.

Sequential Eating: The Ultimate in Food Combining

As you can see, following the traditional rules of food combining will improve your digestion and overall health significantly. If you want to go beyond that to the next step and attain even more efficient digestion and even greater health benefits, you'll want to explore sequential eating, what we call the ultimate in food combining. The digestive energy saved by sequential eating can be used for healing purposes, the elimination of body and tissue wastes, mental work, or greater emotional expression.

As Colonel Bradford tells us, when you eat and finish one food at a time before going to the next (sequential eating), your digestion proceeds in a strata formation. Each type of food is digested in the order in which it is eaten, and the specific digestive enzymes needed for the proper digestion of each food are secreted and put to work without interference. (See page 178, "The Rewards of Proper Food Combining.") If you eat sequentially, you can digest a complete meal in a few hours with no discomfort whatsoever.

When patients come to me (Dr. Bass) with digestive problems—aches and pains in the stomach, gas, constant belching, sour stomach, constipation, or diarrhea—I usually begin by recommending that they give up conventional foods and switch to foods of higher quality. I tell them to avoid highly-cooked foods and packaged snacks, and move toward a predominantly raw diet of vegetables, nuts, seeds, and fruits. But some patients absolutely refuse to give up the foods they are used to eating. Rather than discharge them outright as hopeless cases, I suggest that initially they simply change the order and sequence in which they eat these foods. Within one week, many of the digestive problems of these patients vanish! As you might imagine, they are quite happy with the results. After experiencing this improved digestion, many patients then make further alterations in the quality of their diet.

I improve my patients' diets to the extent that they are willing and able to follow my advice. But my fundamental recommendation is to eat foods in sequential order. Once patients experience improved digestion, increased absorption of nutrients, and overall "good feelings" as a result of sequential eating, they are then more apt to improve the quality of the food they eat as well.

Weight loss is one big benefit of sequential eating, which causes excess pounds to quickly melt away! Think about it. When each mouthful consists of a different or alternating variety of food, the appetite is constantly stimulated, and this leads to the consumption of far more food than is needed to meet the body's requirements. With sequential eating, even while living on a conventional, low-quality diet, you'll lose weight because you'll naturally eat less!

The Principles of Sequential Eating Summarized

Contrary to popular opinion, food does not co-mingle in the stomach unless it's eaten that way. When you eat one food at a time, the food remains layered in the stomach, and it is digested one layer at a time.

In Dr. William Howell's *Textbook of Physiology*, we learn that "Dr. Grutzner (a European researcher) successively fed to rats morsels of food of different colors. After a short period the animals were sacrificed, and the stomach frozen and sectioned. The colored materials were found to be in layers."

Another famous case that corroborates digestion by layer was written about during the American Civil War by a famous physician named Dr. Beaumont. In this case, a soldier received a gunshot wound which caused a large visible opening in his stomach. His digestion was studied for a period of time by several doctors and they observed that his food was digested in successive layers.

If you'd like to demonstrate this for yourself, try eating in sequence watermelon, salad, and cheese. Completely consume each item before moving to the next for several different meals. Then when nature calls, examine the stools and observe different layers of color in the feces. Watermelon, reddish in color, will come first; very dark brown tossed salad will come next; and cheese, very light tan in color, will come last. The waste from each food exits the body in the same order in which it was eaten. Anyone can try this test, but you must eat the different foods one at a time in sequence.

When you consume your foods one at a time, digestion proceeds differently in each strata, or layer, within the stomach. The secretions of digestive enzymes from the stomach wall are different for each layer, and, consequently, all foods are digested much more efficiently.

Let me put to you very simply a key principle of Natural Hygiene: Eat the most watery food first, the next most watery food second, and so on. Finish your meal with the least watery and most concentrated food. NEVER reverse this order of eating.

The concept of sequential eating is reinforced in the advice given by Colonel Bradford. When you eat a meal in sequence, you essentially consume a mono-diet of one food at a time, which Colonel Bradford encouraged. Animals and primates who eat mono-diets achieve the essence of simplicity in digestion.

Here are simple guidelines to follow for proper sequential eating:

1. Begin your meal with the most watery food, and end your meal with the least watery.

2. Most beverages will dilute and wash away the enzymes in each layer, causing digestive difficulty, so do not drink with meals.

3. Fruits and vegetables are very compatible at the same meal if you eat them in the proper sequence. Salad vegetables (without oil dressing) should be eaten before fruits for maximum assimilation of minerals.

4. Avoid fruits with meals containing cooked foods, except if you're eating only one meal a day. In this case, eat the fruits before the cooked foods. If fruits are eaten after the cooked

foods—usually a starch, protein, or fatty food—they won't leave the stomach until the previous or longest-digesting food is expelled. If fruit is held up for hours in the stomach after you consume a starch, protein, or fatty food, fermentation is guaranteed. This will produce much gas, bloating, acid, and indigestion. If you eat a sub-acid fruit before a starch, there is usually no difficulty.

If you're eating one meal a day, leave a 20- to 30-minute space between the raw fruit and the cooked vegetable for maximum digestion.

5. Acids or acid fruit should never be consumed after starches.

6. Never consume sugars, syrups, fresh fruit, or dried fruit after starches, proteins, or fatty foods.

7. For conventional eaters, fish can be eaten before or after potatoes because it is digested so rapidly. Potatoes are one-tenth as concentrated as grain foods and are quickly digested. This is one of the exceptions where you may combine protein and starch at a meal.

8. You may combine foods from certain groups at the same course during a meal because they have the same approximate digestion times. For example,

    ◆ Melons may be eaten one after another, one at a time, up to two varieties maximum. Fresh juicy fruits may also be eaten one after another, one at a time, up to three varieties maximum.

    ◆ Succulent raw salad vegetables may be combined together in a tossed salad—such as tomato, various kinds of lettuce, celery, cucumber, and red and green pepper. If desired, other raw vegetables may be added, including sprouts.

Proper Food Combining

Here's an example of a meal eaten properly, assuming no rest between each course:

(a) 8 ounces of carrot, celery, and cucumber juice which requires a digestion time of approximately 15 minutes.

(b) 8 to 12 ounces of two varieties of blended salad (Romaine lettuce, tomato, celery, cucumber, and red or green pepper ground in a blender until the whirlpool forms) which requires a digestion time of approximately 20 minutes.

(c) 12 to 16 ounces of two varieties of melon or fresh juicy fruit (say, one apple and a pear) which requires a digestion time of approximately 30 minutes.

(d) (optional) 1 to 2 ounces of seeds or nuts which requires a digestion time of approximately two to three hours.

In the diagram below you'll see that the vegetable juice occupies **(a)** for 15 minutes, after which it leaves the stomach.

The blended salad occupies **(b)** and exits the stomach in 20 minutes, approximately five minutes after the vegetable juice.

The melon or two varieties of fruit occupy **(c)** for 30 minutes after leaving the stomach, approximately ten minutes after the blended salad.

If you consume the pumpkin or sunflower seeds **(d)**, they'll remain in the stomach for about two and one-half hours, and will leave the stomach after the fruit.

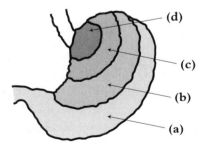

- Steamed or cooked vegetables may be eaten in mixed mouthfuls—first the leafy ones, then the more dense such as zucchini, cauliflower, and broccoli. Follow these with the most dense—the root vegetables such as carrots, rutabagas, beets, and turnips.

- Different kinds of potatoes may be eaten together, followed by sweet potato or yam. Corn may be eaten before a potato, and if eaten raw may be used as a fruit.

- When digestion is sturdy, you may mix grains as desired. A small amount of legume may also follow a grain with good compatibility. For example, if you eat 4 ounces of rice (dry weight), you may add 1 ounce of lentils (dry weight).

- When eating seeds, two varieties may be mixed, such as sunflower plus pumpkin or sesame. Two varieties of nuts may be eaten in sequence on occasion, but one variety is best. Soaking the nuts or seeds overnight in water makes them easier to digest, especially if ground before eating.

- If eating fish, two to three varieties may be eaten together. Two kinds of poultry or meat may be mixed as well, but remember, unnecessary variety leads to overeating and should be avoided. Eat only one starch or protein at a meal.

Dr. Bass's Three Meal Plan

Eat A, B, C, and D (all four) in sequence as written. Finish A before going to B, finish B before beginning C, and so on. Note: Each meal is completely balanced and contains all the nutritional elements needed for good health.

Breakfast

(A) Vegetable juice: ⅓ each of carrot, celery, and cucumber to make 8 ounces of juice.

(B) Blended salad: 8 to 12 ounces of a combination of tomato, Romaine lettuce, cucumber, celery, and/or pepper if desired.

(C) Melon: ⅛ to ¼ of a watermelon for a total of 16 ounces. You may substitute two varieties of fruit other than watermelon or 2 to 4 bananas for a total of 16 ounces.

(D) Choose a combination of the following for a total of 8 to 16 ounces: 1 to 2 soft-boiled egg yolks, 1 ounce raw seeds or nuts, 4 ounces by dry weight of a cooked grain, such as oatmeal, millet, brown rice, or buckwheat, potato, yam, corn, squash. Egg yolks are preferable to nuts or seeds.

Note: Add (D) for physical workers or if on a transitional diet (changing over from a conventional diet to a Natural Hygiene diet). During summer when your body needs additional fluids, you may have increased quantities of melon alone for breakfast.

Lunch

(A) Vegetable juice: ⅓ each of carrot, celery, and cucumber to make 8 ounces of juice.

(B) Blended salad: 8 to 12 ounces or large tossed salad.

(C) One fruit (8 ounces) or 1 to 2 raw ears of corn.

(D) Raw seeds or nuts (1 to 2 ounces) *or* avocado (8 ounces), *or* two times a week, instead of nuts, you may have 8 ounces of ricotta cheese, pot cheese, low-fat cottage cheese (unsalted), or unsalted raw milk cheese (hard, like cheddar or muenster, 2 to 4 ounces). Those who aren't vegetarians may have fish two times a week.

DINNER

(A) Tomato, cucumber, and zucchini juice (8 ounces total).

(B) Tossed salad (8 to 12 ounces) and 1 tablespoon cold-pressed oil and lemon dressing (1 teaspoon lemon juice).

(C) One to two steamed vegetables (4 ounces each).

(D) Choose any two of the following: one ear of corn or squash plus potato, or potatoes plus yam (16 ounces maximum total). Three days a week alternate with grains as follows: On days 1, 3, 5, and 7 have one ear of corn or squash plus potato, or potatoes plus yam (16 ounces maximum total).
On days 2, 4, and 6 have after (A), (B), and (C) 3 to 4 ounces (dry weight) of brown rice, millet or buckwheat plus 1 ounce (dry weight) of lima beans, lentils, or chickpeas.

For non-vegetarians and meat eaters, omit (D) for dinner, and, after having (A), (B), and (C) you may have one potato or 8 to 12 ounces cooked weight of brown rice, millet, buckwheat, or other grain, followed by 4 ounces of fish, chicken, meat, or turkey. Do not eat animal foods more than five times a week at the beginning and then taper off to two or three times a week within a month.

You may have fish two to three times a week, or substitute chicken once a week. Two eggs may be used occasionally in place of chicken.

When eating out socially, conventional eaters may have a tossed salad, then potato, followed by fish or chicken. In a Chinese restaurant, you may have vegetables, then fish, followed by rice. Vegetarians may omit the animal food and have more vegetables followed by rice.

If you want to lose weight, go on a two-meal-a-day plan.

Omit the breakfast or lunch, but include the dinner. Excess pounds will literally disappear! If you are eating only raw foods, replace the above evening meal with a lunch meal. (You'll have one lunch meal for lunch, and another lunch meal for dinner.) Be sure to change the lunch main dish (D) daily. Include a breakfast as one of your three meals.

If you are unable to give up your current, more traditional diet, it is still possible for you to avoid much of the undesirable consequences of chaotic food combinations. Simply follow the basic rule of sequential eating: Eat the most liquid food first and end with the most solid and concentrated food. However, the wise person will endeavor to live as intelligently as possible on the best quality food, the best order of sequential eating, and the correct quantity of food. What is the correct quantity of food? It is the minimum amount you need to get all the essential nutrients necessary for a long, healthful, joyous life, free from disease and infirmity. Many nutritional sages advise us to eat one-third less than we usually eat; other experts urge us to push away from the table while still hungry. Colonel Bradford reminds us that the lamas ate little and lived well on a minimal diet.

Common Questions About Food Combining

How do I take my vitamin supplements and combine properly?
If you follow the guidelines in this chapter and stay on a completely plant-based diet, your body will no longer need supplements other than perhaps Vitamin B_{12} a couple of times a week. Although some authorities claim vegetarians can produce ample B_{12} in the intestinal tract, others disagree and encourage supplementing B_{12} from an outside source.

Won't I starve my body for protein if I don't eat meat?
Study after study by medical researchers and physiologists prove

beyond the shadow of a doubt that Westerners consume far too much protein and this contributes to many of our health ills, including osteoporosis, arthritis, and colon cancer. By not eating meat, you'll also stop poisoning your body with all the antibiotics and growth hormones (and who knows what else) modern flesh farmers stuff into their poor animals to force weight on them and get them to the slaughter houses as quickly as possible.

You can get all the protein you need from three or four ounces of raw, unsalted nuts a day. Or if you follow Colonel Bradford's advice, from two softly cooked egg yolks each day.

You say not to drink milk or eat dairy products. What'll I do for calcium?
Studies reveal that you can get all the calcium your body needs from a plant-based diet. Concentrate on plenty of dark green leafy vegetables, raw nuts and seeds, grains, beans, fresh fruit, dried fruit, vegetables such as broccoli and string beans, and fish such as sardines and salmon.

How will my cholesterol be affected by this way of eating?
Your cholesterol level will drop through the floor when you get away from meat and dairy products and start eating a predominantly plant- and grain-based diet. Some doctors will tell you to swallow pills for the rest of your life to lower your cholesterol and/or your blood pressure. Try a plant-based diet for a few weeks instead along with the Five Rites and perhaps a little brisk walking each day. You'll save the money you would have spent on pills and won't have to suffer any of the horrible side effects.

You'll notice that egg yolks are recommended in this diet. They contain lecithin, which prevents cholesterol from being deposited in your arteries.

Shouldn't I take my foods from the traditionally recommended four food groups or the U.S.D.A.'s new food pyramid? Your diets don't follow these standards at all!

Right, and neither do the diets or lifestyles recommended by Physicians for Responsible Medicine, a group of thousands of medical doctors around the world who decry the U.S. Department of Agriculture's caving in to the powerful Washington lobbies of the meat and dairy industries.

A quick trip to any local library for books by respected medical authorities like Drs. John McDougall, Dean Ornish, and Michael Klaper will prove to any thinking person once and for all that meat and dairy products have contributed to disease and ill health. Read Dr. Neal Bernard's *Food for Life* and learn how the "real" Four Food Groups (fruits, vegetables, grains, legumes) scientifically support a vegetarian lifestyle as the most healthful way of eating. Or check out *Doctor Dean Ornish's Program for Reversing Heart Disease*. Or tackle what some call the definitive vegetarian diet book — *The McDougall Plan for Superhealth and Life-long Weight Loss*.

I'm past 60. Will food combining reverse the effects of my entire lifetime of poor eating habits?

Probably not, but you'll definitely see improvements. Hygiene teaches that results don't occur overnight. Unlike many in the medical profession, Natural Hygiene rejects quick fixes. Instead, Hygiene teaches that the body will heal itself over time when provided with the proper conditions: proper diet, exercise, sleep and rest, and the other Hygienic touchstones described earlier. Once you start combining your plant-based foods with these important elements, you'll notice improvements in your digestion. Gas, indigestion, constipation, heartburn, and other uncomfortable digestive problems will dramatically lessen or disappear completely. Some people also experience vast improvements in chronic conditions, but Hygiene does not come with guarantees. A lifetime of wrong living cannot always be completely reversed by a few years of right living, but it can be greatly improved in all cases.

Should children combine their foods? Is there anyone who wouldn't benefit from food combining?
If your child suffers from gas, heartburn, indigestion, or constipation, food combining and sequential eating might help alleviate or end these problems. But if you feed your family a predominantly plant-based diet, you probably don't have to burden your child with food combining rules because good digestion occurs with natural foods. Unlike an adult with impaired digestion who has guzzled soft drinks and chowed-down on junk foods for years, a child hasn't ruined his or her digestive system with years of improper eating and combining. Mealtime should be a happy time for kids (and for adults) and not a time for scolding, rule-setting, and creating tension. If you serve foods in proper sequence, children will quickly form the right habits without undue discussion.

Will food combining work for people with specific health problems or conditions like high blood pressure, diabetes, hypoglycemia, ulcers, and so on?
Most people will benefit from proper food combining and will notice a decrease in indigestion, gas, and heartburn. Period.

But if you have a medical condition that concerns you, check with a professional health advisor before making any changes in your diet or lifestyle. If you feel uncomfortable with the idea of food combining, consult a health professional knowledgeable in the field of alternative nutrition. Most medical doctors and traditionally-educated nutritionists know little about food combining, vegetarian nutrition, or superior health. The majority of American medical students, for example, devote fewer than three hours to nutritional studies. Their schools and mentors teach them about disease and the alleviation of symptoms through drugs. The current medical model does not teach about natural remedies for health problems and the body's power to heal itself. Ironically, as a group, medical doctors die at a younger age than many other groups of people.

So look for a health advisor who specializes in "true" health when you want professional advice regarding food combining or nutrition.

I overeat all too often. Can you give me guidelines on how much I should be eating for maximum health?
It is the minimum amount of the best quality of food you can get that provides all the essential nutrients necessary for a long, healthful, joyous life, free from disease and infirmity. Leave the table hungry. Eat at least ⅓ less food than you're used to eating at each meal. Skip a meal several times a week. Don't snack. Don't eat anything after 7:00 p.m. Remember that Luigi Cornaro, the Italian Renaissance writer, lived on 12 ounces of food and 14 ounces of grape juice a day! You probably shouldn't try that kind of minimal diet, but you can live on a lot less than what you're living on now. (See the Three-Meal Plan beginning on page 197 for maximum amounts of each food.)

Can I expect any discomfort or side effects as I make the transition to proper food combining?
Most people will notice vast improvements in their digestion when they start food combining. After a time, however, particularly if you move to a plant-based diet, you will probably go through a period when you come down with a cold or experience headaches, stomachaches, or flu-like symptoms. Instead

of running to the doctor for a pill, ride with the experience for a few days.

When your body reacts this way, it is simply cleaning out some of the toxins and poisons from years of less-than-superior living and eating habits. When detoxing, take to bed. Drink distilled water when thirsty, eat as little as possible (stick to citrus fruit and fresh vegetable juices if you must have something), sleep as much as you can in a well-ventilated and naturally-lighted room, and enjoy your time away from the rat race for a few days.

Once your body finishes this cleansing process, you may feel the best you've felt in years!

Will you summarize the basic principles of food combining for me?

1. The smaller the amount of a particular food eaten, the less the digestive time for that food. The greater the amount, the greater the digestive time, and the more energy needed for digestion.

2. The more thoroughly you chew your food, the quicker it is digested.

3. The less you mix and the fewer the varieties of food you eat at one time, the easier it is to digest and the less you will be tempted to overeat. The greater the variety, the greater the tendency to overeat.

4. And finally, follow Colonel Bradford's excellent advice and move at your own pace! The Romans didn't build Rome in a day, and you can't expect to gain superior health in a week. Pace yourself and move slowly and comfortably. By practicing the Five Rites and food combining, you will experience the best health you've had in years!

In addition to providing advice on diet and nutrition, Colonel Bradford also offered teachings on the importance of sound and the voice to one's health and longevity. In the next chapter, we will look at these teachings.

Dr. Stanley S. Bass has been an alternative health physician and nutritionist for almost fifty years. Dr. Bass earned his Doctor of Naturopathy degree from the American School of Naturopathy, and later became a Diplomat in Naturopathy. He also earned a degree in nutrition from the New York Institute of Dietetics and a Doctor of Chiropractic from the Columbian College of Chiropractic.

Dr. Bass is available for phone consultations and by appointment for personal visits. He has written numerous books and articles on Natural Hygiene and sensible, healthful living. You can obtain a list of his publications by writing Dr. Stanley S. Bass, 3119 Coney Island Ave., Brooklyn, NY 11235, or you can call him at (718) 648-1500.

Medical researcher and journalist Chet Day writes about Natural Hygiene, health-building through all-natural means, and plant-based diets in his monthly newsletter, Health & Beyond. Day also publishes a variety of booklets on healthful living and writes articles for various alternative health publications.

Learn more about Day's work by requesting your free Natural Health Resource Guide from Chet Day, 4258 Stafford Drive, Winter Haven, FL 33880-1141, via computer at his chetday@aol.com e-mail address, or by telephone at (941) 294-0300.

CHAPTER SEVEN

Energetics of the Voice, Sound, and Meditation

by Richard Leviton

When he first returned from India, Colonel Bradford impressed the people he knew as the "image of perfection." After many more months of steady application of the Five Rites and the lifestyle teachings he had learned in Tibet, the Colonel made even more impressive gains in vigor, alertness, and general youthfulness. The secret had to do with new teachings on sound and the voice, specifically, the male voice.

For those whose ears are trained to listen, the quality of a man's voice — its pitch, timbre, and vibration — reveals his sexual vitality, and this indicates the quality and quantity of his life force energy, which Colonel Bradford calls *prana*, and the Chinese call *Qi* (pronounced *chee*). When a man's voice is full of prana, it is deep and resonant, and sounds full-bodied, explains Colonel Bradford. The shrill, piping voice of an elderly man is a certain sign that he is physically declining.

To explain the relationship between voice, life force energy, and physical decline, we must look at the model of the energy centers called *chakras* (see Chapter Four). There is a distinct energetic relationship between the fifth chakra, your throat center, the seat of the larynx and vocal cords, and your sexual center, the first chakra. As Bradford explains, these two centers, representing the functions of speaking and procreating, are "geared together." What affects one center mutually affects the other, creating a strong connection between sexual vitality and the quality of the spoken voice. When you hear a man with a high and shrill voice, you can be fairly certain that his sexual vitality and the energy level in the first chakra are low; in fact it's highly likely that the energy in his other centers is similarly deficient.

What's the remedy? Consciously make an effort to keep your voice low, advises Colonel Bradford, and try to intensify the vibratory quality of your voice. "Before long, the lowered vibration of your voice will speed up the vortex in the base of the throat," says Bradford. And that will quicken the spin of the sexual center "which is the body's doorway to vital life energy." This in turn will move Qi, or prana, upward through the other centers and enliven the throat center. For younger men, this practice will preserve virility, while for older men, it will renew it.

As with a man, a woman's voice can become too high and shrill with physical decline. While a woman should attempt to "tone down" her voice in the same manner that a man would, she should not "lower her voice to the point of sounding masculine," says Colonel Bradford. A woman's voice is naturally higher-pitched than a man's and should remain so. "In fact," says Bradford, "it would be beneficial for a woman whose voice is abnormally masculine to attempt to raise her voice in pitch."

The Tibetan monks Colonel Bradford met in his travels used chanting as a powerful tool for lowering the voice. "The lamas chant in unison, sometimes for hours, in a low register. The significance of this is not the chanting itself or the meaning of the chant's words. It is the vibration of their voices and its effect on the seven vortexes," says Colonel Bradford. Since the Colonel's time, Tibetan monks have become world famous and widely admired among Western Buddhists and musicologists for their extraordinary ability to chant in the lowest possible registers of the voice. They chant so deeply it's as if their voices were sounding from underneath all the rocks in the Earth.

One particular sound the lamas chant is especially effective. "When intoned correctly," explains Bradford, "it has a very powerful stimulating effect on the pineal gland, which is related to the seventh and highest vortex." However, cautions Bradford, the pineal gland should not receive so much stimulation unless the individual has begun to focus on consciousness of a higher order.

The sound is *OM* (*Oh-h-h-M-m-m*), and because it is so powerful, Bradford warned against "overdoing a good thing." Repeating three or four times in succession, he says, is sufficient. And, he added, it is not the meaning of the word or the act of chanting that is important, but the sound vibration of the voice — the energetics of the voice.

In this chapter, we'll look at the matter of voice energetics. As we discovered in earlier chapters when we looked into the traditions Bradford drew on, there is a great deal of material both in the Tibetan tradition and in Western teachings that not only supports Bradford's claims but expands them and teases out their riches. We'll see that the voice — not only the male voice, but the female voice as well — is a powerful tool that is not limited by gender. We'll consider the nature of sound, vibration, chanting, and how these relate to the chakras in the Eastern tradition. We'll also look at the healing powers of the voice through special practices called toning and vocal harmonics, and we'll note some surprising relationships between the throat center and the sexual chakra.

First, let's begin with a practical exercise that will enable you to link sounds with the energy centers. Later we'll add colors. As we move along, we'll fill in some of the ideas that support these practices.

How to Sound Your Energy Centers

Buddhist and Hindu teachers have always linked sounds with the energy centers. In recent years, Westerners working with the healing properties of sound and music have adapted these teachings and presented them in a practical format. One such musicologist and music therapist is Jonathan Goldman, author of *Healing Sounds: The Power of Harmonics*. Goldman believes strongly in the therapeutic power of the human voice. In his seminars, he teaches participants how to practice what he calls vocal harmonics, making vowel sounds and sending them to the various energy centers. Doing this, he explains, enables you to actually resonate any part of your body or energy center through the power of your voice. In addition, when you use your voice to produce vowel sounds, you begin to change the way your voice sounds and this starts to change the quality of your consciousness, Goldman says. Colonel Bradford would certainly agree.

Here is an exercise developed by Jonathan Goldman that uses your voice and specific vowel sounds to stimulate your energy centers. You can practice it every day as a quick chakra toneup after you have finished the Five Rites. It should take you perhaps 15 minutes and will be remarkably relaxing and energizing. Begin by following these steps:

- Find a quiet room that is adequately lighted.
- Sit comfortably in a straight-backed chair with your feet flat on the floor and a couple of inches apart. It is best to remove your shoes and socks; if you wear glasses, remove

them. Rest your hands in your lap. You may close your eyes if you wish.

- Breathe naturally several times through your nose until you feel relaxed.
- Be sure to follow the steps for each energy center to complete the exercise. (See Chapter Four to locate each energy center.)

SOUNDING YOUR ROOT CENTER

- Make your first sound. Pitching your voice as deeply as possible, make the sound *Uh*. Say it as you breathe out. Make this sound at your normal speaking volume or quieter if you prefer.
- As you make the sound *Uh*, place your attention on your root chakra, which is in your groin at your perineum. As you breathe out, make the sound *Uh* as if you were sitting in your root center. You will feel the *Uh* sound resonating in your throat, but imagine that it is vibrating the area of your root center at the base of your spine.
- Make this sound every time you breathe out for one minute, then stop and relax.

SOUNDING YOUR SACRAL CENTER

- Now move your attention up the spine to your second chakra, the sacral center. This one is located at the area of your pubic region or about three inches below the navel.
- Make the sound *Ooo* (rhymes with too) as you breathe out. Pitch this *Ooo* sound a little higher than the way you sounded *Uh*. As before, try to feel this sound vibrating in your pubic area through the second energy center. Do this for a minute, then stop and relax.

Sounding Your Solar Plexus Center

- Find the third energy center, the solar plexus chakra, above your navel. It extends from the base of your sternum to your navel.
- Focus your attention here as you breathe out and make the sound *Oh*. Make the *Oh* sound a little higher in pitch than you did for *Ooo*; this would put it at about the middle range of your voice. Do this for a minute, then stop and relax.

Sounding Your Heart Center

- Now move your attention up to the heart center, your fourth chakra, which is located in the chest area essentially between the shoulder blades and the bottom of the rib cage.
- As you focus on this center, make the sound *Ah* at a pitch a little higher than you did for *Oh*. Feel this sound resonating throughout your chest cavity. Do this for a minute, then stop and relax.

Sounding Your Throat Center

- Your throat center, the fifth chakra, sits at the center of your throat. Basically, you may consider all of your neck to be the throat chakra. With your attention focused here, make the sound *Eye* at a pitch somewhat higher than you did for *Ah*. Feel the sound Eye vibrating in your throat causing the petals of the chakra to flutter as if brushed by a gentle breeze. Do this for a minute, then stop and relax.

Sounding Your Brow Center

- The next energy center is located between your eyebrows, which is why it is commonly known as the brow chakra (also known as the third eye chakra). Here you breathe out and make the sound *Ay*. Visualize the *Ay* sound vibrating inside your brow energy center. Do this for a minute, then stop and relax.

SOUNDING YOUR CROWN CENTER

♦ Finally, make the sound *Eee* for your crown center at the top of your head. Chakra experts tell us this center is like a lotus flower with one thousand petals. Visualize that as you make the sound *Eee*, it vibrates throughout this thousand-petalled flower and makes all the petals flutter. Do this for a minute, then stop and relax.

This completes the exercise for sounding your energy centers. You may feel slightly light-headed. This is natural and will pass in a few minutes. Continue breathing calmly through your nose. If you wish, you can reverse the exercise and proceed down the chakra column, making the sounds for the crown, brow, throat, heart, navel, sexual center, and root chakra in that order. Or you may open your eyes, look around, rub your hands, and stand up.

It is important to have the right intention when you practice these sounds. Your conscious intent—a positive, loving affirmation of your potential to heal—is essential for good results, Goldman stresses. One of the first things he tells his students is this simple but potent formula: Frequency plus intent produces healing. Try to be aware of the vibrational effects, both physiological and psychological, of the sounds you are making to ensure that you get their maximum benefit.

Toning: A Quick Way to Energize Your Body with Your Voice

Toning is an even simpler but equally effective way to use your voice to send energy through your energy centers. It's a kind of free-form use of your voice. The therapeutic application of toning has been gaining momentum for decades ever since Laurel Elizabeth Keyes, a pastoral counselor working in Denver, Colorado, discovered her "natural body voice" through an act of spontaneous, cathartic toning after a workshop in the 1960s.

Standing alone in the seminar room Keyes noticed a sensation in her throat and chest, "as though a force were rising, wanting to be released in sound." The force had its own volition; when it erupted through her voice into a myriad of sounds, it soared like a bird that had been caged all its life, flying "in delighted abandonment, effortlessly, free as artesian water flows from the ground," said Keyes. It wasn't her personal voice, but rather the voice of her physical body, expressed only now for the first time, liberated from mental direction and emotional suppression. "Each time I toned," explained Keyes, "my body felt exhilarated, alive, as it had never felt before. It appeared to cleanse the entire body, releasing tensions and congested areas." A psychic told Keyes the tone was like a swirling movement around her uterus that drew up magnetic currents from the earth through the feet and limbs, rising in a spiral of light before release through the throat.

Toning assists healing from the inside out, said Keyes, who devoted the rest of her life to teaching people to tone for self-healing until her death in 1983. For good health, we should take a "tone bath" every day, letting our voice "express its freedom."

Toning for Self-Healing

Toning is an exercise you can practice after your daily session of doing the Five Rites. You might do it after the previous exercise ("Stimulating Your Energy Centers") or instead of it, alternating them every other day. This exercise is best practiced standing up while you are alone. Since you will be making unusual, spontaneous sounds, it is best if you can practice this in a space in which you feel safe and private.

Follow these steps for healing through toning:

- Stand up straight with your feet several inches apart. Close your eyes but keep your attention vigilant.
- Be aware of your breathing as your breath moves in then out of your body.
- Be open to the idea that your body has sounds it wants to make, that your body wants to speak through sound. You have to trust yourself that this is not silly, stupid, or embarrassing. Consider it an experiment.
- Perhaps your body wants to groan. Try making a groaning sound that begins in your feet and moves up your torso. Let the sound waver and build, peak and fall as it wants to. There are no rules in toning.
- Allow the sound to go where it wishes, to be as loud, quiet, harsh, gentle, musical, or discordant as it wishes. This free-form sound will energetically sweep your chakras and sonically cleanse them. Most likely you will feel a sigh after perhaps a few minutes of toning.

Here is another toning exercise. In this routine you turn your voice into a siren and use it to sweep your body with sound. You literally copy the sound of a siren with your voice.

- Stand up erect with your feet spread apart and your eyes closed.
- Start low then gradually build the pitch until you are making a sound at the top of your voice.
- Gradually come down the scale to the lowest sound you can make. As you do this, imagine you are sweeping your body and energy centers with sound. The lowest sound sweeps through your lower trunk and root center.
- Build the sounds up again as they move through your

energy centers until you reach your crown chakra. Here is the topmost pitch of your voice siren.

- Come down the scale again as the siren descends in pitch. Imagine the sounds sweeping down through your body to your feet again.
- After you have finished, sit down and rest for a few minutes.

In addition to using toning as a self-healing technique, Keyes also developed the "body-voice siren scan," a technique used today by music therapists who use their own voice as a diagnostic tool for clients. The therapist starts toning from the feet, using the modulations in her own voice to scan the energetic condition of the client's body. Knowing that every pain has a specific tone, Keyes said, "When the sound returns to me from the afflicted area, I know it." She described the sensation as characteristically "sticky and thick."

The client then concentrates on the distressed area identified by the therapist as the therapist rhythmically pulsates the exact sound she senses in that body region "until (her) body sighs," as Keyes described it. This tells her the congestion is broken up. She completes the vocal scan on a high note at the client's head.

Surely Colonel Bradford would agree with Keyes's general view: "The tone of a person's voice is highly indicative of his state, not only of health but of affairs. By the manner in which we speak, every hour of our lives, we set the pattern for our lives."

The Power of Mantras to Unlock Your Energy Centers

When he discussed the subject of mantras, Colonel Bradford—who used the term mantram to denote a spoken mantra—treated these sounds or spoken phrases as personal affirmations. But in Buddhist and Hindu traditions, mantras are carefully chosen sound combinations given to a student by a meditation master, to be repeated as often as possible. Perhaps the most familiar to Westerners is the famous one from Buddhism, *OM mane padme hum*! As mentioned earlier, Bradford observed Tibetan monks chanting very deeply-pitched sounds, including the sound *OM* (pronounced *Oh-h-h-M-m-m-m-m-m*).

In Indian Hindu traditions *Aum*—the written equivalent of Tibet's *OM*—has an awesome cosmic resonance. It is a profoundly sacred sound: the seed syllable or *bija* of the universe itself. And since Buddhism came to Tibet by way of India, *Aum* is central to any study of Tibetan mysticism. Its three elements (A-u-m) represent the three basic states of consciousness: waking, dream, and deep sleep. Aum, as a whole, represents cosmic consciousness that encompasses everything in creation. As Indian poet Rabindranath Tagore expresses it, "*Aum* is the symbolic word for the infinite, the perfect, the eternal." This surely helps us see why Colonel Bradford recommended that his Himalaya Club members utilize *OM* when ready to progress to higher states of consciousness.

Practicing Mantras to Stimulate Your Energy Centers

Here is a simple exercise that puts the principle of mantras (or mantrams) to work. As with the others, you can practice it after you finish your daily round of doing the Five Rites and as part of a set of routines dealing with sound.

- Sit comfortably in a straight-backed chair with your feet flat on the floor and a couple of inches apart. It is best to remove your shoes and socks; if you wear glasses, remove them.
- Rest your hands in your lap. You may close your eyes if you wish.

- Breathe naturally several times through your nose until you feel relaxed.
- Focus on your root center. As you breathe out make the sound *Lam* (pronounced *lahm*, rhymes with *Guam*). Let your breath carry it out of your mouth.
- Now move to your second energy center at the pubic bone. As you breathe out make the sound *Vam* (pronounced *vahm*); repeat this 12 times.
- At the solar plexus, do *Ram* (pronounced *rahm*) 12 times; at the heart, *Yam* (pronounced *yahm*) 12 times; at the throat, *Ham* (pronounced *hahm*) 12 times. At the brow center, make the sound *OM* (pronounced *Oh-h-h-M-m-m-m*) 12 times.

There is no sound for the crown center because it is the combined sound of the lower six centers. When you have completed this set, try practicing the entire mantra, *OM mane padme hum!* (pronounced *Ohh-mmm, mahn-ee pahd-mee hooom!*). Do this in as deep a voice as you can, pronouncing all the syllables in a single breath. Repeat this 5 times, then relax.

The Sounds of the Chakra Petals Spell the Sanskrit Alphabet

At this point you may well wonder how sounds can affect the energy centers. There is a profound reason your voice can have a healing, even transformative effect on the chakras, and through them, on your mind and body. The secret is the Sanskrit alphabet.

We know that the seven chakras each have a different number of petals. There are 4 in the root, 6 in the sacral, 10 in the solar plexus, 12 in the heart, 16 in the throat, 2 in the brow (although each is said to contain 48 minor petals, giving this center 96), and 1,000 in the crown (see Chapter Four). We also know, if we have seen any of the standard pictures of the chakras, that each of these petals has a Sanskrit letter written on it. What does this mean?

The Sanskrit alphabet, widely regarded as one of the world's oldest and preeminent sacred tongues and the source of numerous mantras, is comprised of 50 letters. Each of these letters is really a sound. The number of chakra petals for the first six chakras is also 50, and on each of these petals a different Sanskrit letter/sound is inscribed. According to Sanskrit expert Vyaas Houston, director of the American Sanskrit Institute in Warwick, New York, and a Sanskrit educator with 20 years of experience, this means that the 50 letters/sounds of the Sanskrit alphabet essentially create, form, and activate the 50 petals of the first six chakras, from root to brow. That's why, as a kind of open secret, the vowels and consonants of Sanskrit are displayed on the individual petals of the six chakras. Your chakras are made of sound.

In the vibratory alphabet that is Sanskrit, the sounds are the petals and chakras themselves. For example, the Sanskrit petal sounds for the root chakra are *Vang, Shang, Kshang, Sang*; for the sacral center, they are *Bang, Bhang, Mang, Yang, Rang*, and *Lang*. This means that when you speak these sounds—more precisely, when you intone them through proper vocal technique—you make the sound that actually creates the petals of the particular chakra. On an energy level, when you say *Vang, Shang, Kshang,* and *Sang*, you are recreating the four-petal structure of the root chakra. So it makes sense for somebody wishing to stimulate the chakras to chant their Sanskrit sounds.

Certainly these remarkable insights help us better understand why Colonel Bradford assured his students that an energized, deepened, and intensified voice was so important. Now we can see how the throat chakra can have a such a strong effect on the vortex spin and energetic quality of the four lower centers.

Rainbow Chakras:
Experiencing Your Energy Centers through Color

In addition to specific sounds, each chakra is associated with a different color. Your root center is associated with the color red, or scarlet; your sacral center with the color orange; your solar plexus is associated with the color yellow; your heart center with green; your throat center with blue; your brow center with indigo; and your crown center with violet. By visualizing a specific color for each center, you can experience the energy of your chakras in another way.

Here is a meditative exercise involving your chakras, this time using the element of color. You can practice it every day after you have finished the Five Rites. It should take you 10 minutes and can be both relaxing and energizing.

Follow the same format as you did with the earlier exercise, "How to Sound Your Energy Centers." Begin with these steps:

- Find a quiet room that is adequately lighted.
- Sit comfortably in a straight-backed chair with your feet flat on the floor and a couple of inches apart. It is best to remove your shoes and socks; if you wear glasses, remove them.
- Rest your hands in your lap. You may close your eyes if you wish.
- Breathe naturally several times through your nose until you feel relaxed.
- Be sure to follow the steps for each energy center to complete the exercise.

COLORING YOUR ROOT CENTER
- Visualize your first color. As you breathe out, imagine that you are breathing out the color red or scarlet. Focus

your attention on your root center which is in your groin at your perineum. Include your torso from the groin to your feet in this color.

- Every time you breathe out, pretend you are spray painting your root center scarlet-red. Feel the warmth of this bright color.
- In this manner, breathe this color into your root center for one minute, then stop and relax.

COLORING YOUR SACRAL CENTER

- Now move your attention up the spine to your second energy center. This one is located at the area of your pubic region, or about three inches below the navel.
- Visualize the color orange in the area of your pubic bone. Be sure to include both the front and back of your body at this region, as if you are tying an orange color band around you.
- Every time you breathe out, breathe the color orange to this energy center. Feel the warmth of this bright color.
- In this manner, breathe this color into your sacral center for one minute, then stop and relax.

COLORING YOUR SOLAR PLEXUS CENTER

- Find the third energy center at your navel. This is called the solar plexus chakra and occupies the region from the base of your sternum to the navel. Focus your attention here as you visualize the color bright yellow. You might imagine you have captured the sun inside your midriff and it is beaming gloriously from within. Its light irradiates all of your midsection, both front and back. Feel the energizing quality of this bright color.
- Breathe this color into your solar plexus center every time you breathe out for one minute, then stop and relax.

Coloring Your Heart Center

- Now move your attention up to the heart center. This is located in the chest area essentially between the shoulder blades and the bottom of the rib cage. As you focus on this center, visualize the color green. Every time you breathe out visualize your upper thoracic cavity, both front and back, filling with the color green. Feel the calm balancing quality of this color.
- Every time you breathe out, breathe this color into your heart center for one minute, then stop and relax.

Coloring Your Throat Center

- Your throat center sits at the center of your throat. Basically, you may consider the entire neck area to be the throat chakra. With your attention focused here, visualize the color blue as a color band completely around your neck, from the top of your shoulders to the bottom of your head. Make this a rich navy blue.
- Every time you breathe out, fill your throat center with the calming, peaceful color blue.
- In this manner, breathe this color into your throat center for one minute, then stop and relax.

Coloring Your Brow Center

- The next energy center is located between your eyebrows, which is why it is commonly known as the third eye chakra. Every time you breathe out imagine the space between your two eyes filling with the color indigo.
- In this manner, breathe this color into your brow center for one minute, then stop and relax.

Coloring Your Crown Center

- Finally, for the crown center at the top of your head,

visualize that you are filling the center with a rich violet color. As you breathe out, breathe violet to the one thousand petals of your crown center.

- Do this for a minute, then stop and relax.

This completes the exercise for coloring your energy centers. You may feel slightly light-headed; you may feel like a vertical rainbow. You probably have a more direct, experiential connection with the energy feelings of each of your seven chakras.

Continue breathing calmly through your nose. If you wish, you can reverse the exercise and proceed down the chakra column, visualizing the colors again for the crown, brow, throat, heart, solar plexus, sacral and root chakras, in that order. Or you may open your eyes, look around, rub your hands, and stand up.

Practicing the exercises I have described will supplement your work with the Five Rites and provide additional benefits.

Meditating on the Energy Shapes of a Long Life

Many of the new chakra educators working in the West encourage their students to set up a "dialogue" with their energy centers by way of their sound, color, and imagery components (see chart, page 226). We've already sampled some of the results you can expect when you focus on the sound or color aspect of each chakra. Now let's expand this to consider other factors.

According to standard attributions, the root center, for example, has four petals, is associated with the color red and the sense of smell, and the Sanskrit syllable Lam (located in its center). Its geometric figure is a yellow square or cube; its animal is an elephant with seven trunks. And there are several deities including Bala Brahma and Dakini Shakti, who are expressions on a lower plane of the exalted divinities Brahma, Lord of Creation, and Shakti, the Mother of cosmic energy. The whole image becomes a kind of chakra mandala of the energy features of this area of the body and this state of consciousness.

SOUND, COLOR, AND IMAGERY OF THE CHAKRAS					
Chakra	Sound	Color	Shape	Element	Animal
1. Root or Base	Lam	Red	Cube	Earth	Elephant
2. Sacral	Vam	Orange	Crescent	Water	Crocodile
3. Solar Plexus	Ram	Yellow	Triangle	Fire	Ram
4. Heart	Yam	Green	Pentagram	Air	Deer
5. Throat	Ham	Blue	Teardrop	Ether	—
6. Brow	OM	Indigo	—	—	—
7. Crown	—	Violet	—	—	—

Any or all of these elements can be usefully taken as the focus of a meditation. For example, you might visualize the cube as existing in the area of your root center then energize it by focusing your breath and attention upon its elements. While doing so, you might keep in mind that the components of this image may well represent actual doorways into the energetic reality of this center. Although it's hard to understand exactly what's meant by this, the chakra texts teach us that when the basic energy and life issues of a given chakra are mastered, you perceive these fields of life anew. You now appreciate them as the cosmic seats for divine spiritual beings, which is to say, for exalted states of consciousness available to men and women.

A Wheel of Life mandala and the Tibetan monk who painted it. Mandalas
—often used as a focus for meditation—are symbolic, circular images
representing the universe, totality, and completeness.

Photograph by Thomas L. Kelly from Tibet, Reflections from the Wheel of Life, *published by*
Abbeville Press, New York, 1993.

"The body itself becomes a mandala during meditation, and within it there are numerable smaller mandalas, because each center is such a one," Lama Anagarika Govinda, Tibetan Buddhism Scholar, teaches us. Govinda advises that when you use this chakra mandala as a focus for meditation, you should imagine yourself as being at the center of the image, as the embodiment of the divine spiritual figure itself. Such figures represent attainable states of higher consciousness or "perfect Buddhahood."

In this way, the chakras and their mandala-images comprise a kind of cosmic-spiritual temple within your body and in your attention. And since you are dealing with formative forces and immortal spiritual beings, surely the more you identify with these, the more you bring that rarefied energy into your body, right into the physiology of your cells. How can you not feel rejuvenated and energized, knowing you are well on the way to a longer, more vigorous life, just as Colonel Bradford promised.

CHAKRA MANDALA MEDITATION

Let's put this into action with another chakra meditation. You can practice this every day as a quick chakra exercise after you have finished the Five Rites. Be sure to follow the steps for each energy center to complete the exercise. It should take you 10 minutes and will be both relaxing and energizing.

- Find a quiet room that is adequately lighted.
- Sit comfortably in a straight-backed chair with your feet flat on the floor and a couple of inches apart. It is best to remove your shoes and socks; if you wear glasses, remove them.
- Rest your hands in your lap. You may close your eyes if you wish.
- Breathe naturally several times through your nose until you feel relaxed.

MEDITATION FOR YOUR ROOT CENTER

- Starting with your root center, as you exhale, visualize a yellow cube. This cube has six sides, each side is a square, and all sides are yellow. See if you can place yourself inside this yellow cube. Keep breathing the color yellow to this shape. The cube is the symbolic shape of the earth element.

- Now bring to mind the image of an elephant. Imagine that your yellow cube sits on the elephant's back. Feel how strong and solid this cube and elephant are.

- Continue this visualization for one minute, strengthening it every time you breathe out. Then relax, forget about it, and breathe calmly with no other activity.

MEDITATION FOR YOUR SACRAL CENTER

- Now let's move up one notch in the chakra totem pole to the sacral center in the area of your pubic bone. As you breathe out, imagine you are sitting in an upturned white crescent moon, something like a half-circle hammock. This is the symbolic color and shape for the water element, which is all about feelings, relatedness, flow, and change.

- Now visualize that underneath this crescent swims a crocodile. This is not a dangerous crocodile, but one that symbolizes the flowingness of water. Traditionally, Hindu meditators visualize a semi-mythical water animal called a makara, which is an antecedent of the crocodile. Feel the flowingness of the water element as you inhabit the white crescent.

- Continue this visualization for one minute, strengthening it every time you breathe out. Then relax, forget about it, and breathe calmly with no other activity.

MEDITATION FOR YOUR SOLAR PLEXUS CENTER

+ For the solar plexus chakra, visualize an upwards-pointing red triangle. As you breathe out, strengthen this meditative image of a red triangle pointing upwards like a pyramid. This is the symbolic shape for the fire element.

+ Now summon to mind the image of a ram or male sheep. This is the traditional animal associated with the solar plexus center; the feisty, energetic, even combative ram symbolizes the solar energy of this center or the quick burn of the fire element.

+ Continue this visualization for one minute, strengthening it every time you breathe out. Then relax, forget about it, and breathe calmly with no other activity.

MEDITATION FOR YOUR HEART CENTER

+ Now for the heart. As you breathe out, visualize a green pentagram or what is known as the Star of David. This is made of two triangles, one with its point facing upwards, the other with its point facing downwards, forming a six-sided star. The Star of David, in addition to being a primary symbol of the Jewish people, is also an ancient symbol for the balancing function of the heart. Try to imagine yourself sitting inside this pentagram. It is a little like facing up and down at the same time. One triangle is like a pyramid whose cone rises above you; the other triangle is like a pyramid whose cone descends below you.

+ Now visualize a deer. The fleet-footed deer is the symbolic animal for the air element. Thoughts come and go as quickly as a deer darting away through the woods.

+ Continue this visualization for one minute, strengthening it every time you breathe out. Then relax, forget about it, and breathe calmly with no other activity.

- With the throat center we enter the domain of the element of space or ether. Here as you breathe out visualize a pale blue teardrop, as if you are looking at a drop of water close up. Imagine you are sitting inside this blue drop; it is unbelievably spacious and empty.
- Continue this visualization for one minute, strengthening it every time you breathe out. Then relax, forget about it, and breathe calmly with no other activity.

This completes the chakra totem pole of the five elements. No element is associated with the brow and crown chakras; as such, they represent energy states beyond the gravity of matter, which is made of the five elements. In a sense, the place of insight and observation from which you perform this chakra column visualization is set within the brow chakra.

Attributions of shapes and elements to the chakras varies according to different systems. Technically, the Tibetans recognize only five chakras. They combine the second and third, and the brow and crown centers. The Hindus of India work with all seven. The exercises in this chapter recognize seven centers as well. This is partly because the Indian civilization is the source of Tibetan Buddhism and its teachings, and partly because most contemporary chakra educators in the West work with seven centers.

Creative Sounds at the Heart of the Matter

Let us close this chapter with some general reflections on the nature of sound and vibration. Everything is vibration, or, as the ancient Hindus called it, *Nada Brahma*: the world is sound. All of Creation, even emptiness, is vibratory sound. God, or Brahma, the primordial creator and power in the cosmos, is a current of sound and "the inner consciousness of man and of all living things," says musicologist Joachim-Ernst Berendt. "One singularity, the primal sound of being: Being itself—that's Nada Brahma."

Much of reality is hearable, potentially. The rose, upon blossoming, has an audible sound that is like the drone of an organ, according to photo-acoustic spectroscopy. A single corn stalk has a demonstrable sound. Atoms have individual resonating sounds which collectively form chords, or molecules; the atom is a tiny musical note and even a stone is frozen music. All of nature exists in a vast oscillatory spectrum. "It is the song of life *par excellence*, an immense choir, millions and billions of sounds that fuse into a grand polyphony, a harmony beyond human imagination," says Berendt.

Not only does musical sound animate matter but it may well form it, too. That sound shapes matter and imparts structure was unarguably demonstrated by Swiss scientist Hans Jenny in the 1960s. Using electronic sound oscillators and sophisticated photographic equipment, Jenny proved that sound waves underlie matter—a new field he called *cymatics*. He filmed the instantaneous shaping effects of tones, music, and vocal sound on various substances (sand, iron filings, lycopodium powder, water, mercury) spread on a metal plate. Jenny meticulously catalogued the symmetrical, geometrically perfect structures and elegant sound mandalas that resulted from directing hundreds of different frequencies and rhythmic combinations, from single tones and intervals to complex musical harmonies, through the plate.

As the sounds increased in frequency, so did the complexity of the figures generated. Jenny's astonishing images resembled *yantras*, geometrical diagrams used as icons in meditation and often found with pictures of the chakras, as much as with the formation of continents, or the intricate vasculature of a liver cell. In his experiments, the substances on the metal plate kept their structure as long as the specific formative sound continued. For Jenny, this indicated that organic structures in nature, including the tissues, cells, and organs of the human body, must also be profoundly affected by sound wave frequencies. He realized that cymatics was the key to treating disease with sound therapy.

This suggestion was picked up in the 1970s by English osteopath Dr. Peter Guy Manners who developed his unique Cymatic Instrument as a means of delivering therapeutic sound in the range of 60 hz to 30,000 hz to the human body through a hand-held skin-contact applicator. Disease, in Manners's Cymatic model, is caused by a harmonic imbalance in the body's fundamental vibration. This overall body vibration is the sum of numerous interdependent organ, tissue, and molecular vibrations. This means the human body is a great and complex sound resonator comprised of many octaves of biological systems that have the potential to be in a harmonious, musical relationship. This would indicate optimal health.

Health is maintained through regulating the harmonics of the body, said Manners. When the individual harmonics of the heart, liver, spleen, bones, and muscles vibrate in harmony, we are in harmonic pulse and healthy. "But if any part loses its tune or goes out of phase, then we are in trouble until we reproduce those necessary harmonic signals through the Cymatic Instrument to reestablish an organ's innate sound," explained Manners. He and a handful of other Cymatic therapists have worked successfully with conditions such as bone fractures, arthritis, muscle strain, whiplash, slipped discs, fibrositis, paralysis, and rheumatism, but after 20 years he considers the field to still be in its infancy.

In sound, vibration, and the speaking voice we encounter some of the deepest mysteries of the world. All of this helps us see the importance of Colonel Bradford's teachings on the energetics of the voice, how it can stimulate the chakras, and how working with the voice, as well as color and other elements, can enhance the benefits of the Five Rites.

Richard Leviton has been a natural health journalist for 20 years. He was Senior Writer for East West Journal (now Natural Health), Yoga Journal, and The Quest, and he is the author of numerous books, including The Imagination of Pentecost *(Anthroposophic Press, 1994),* Brain Builders *(Prentice Hall, 1995), and* Looking for Arthur *(Station Hill Press, 1995). Richard is currently Executive Editor of* Alternative Medicine Digest *and Future Medicine Publishing.*

CHAPTER EIGHT

A Conversation with Dr. Robert Thurman

by Laura Faye Taxel

D*r. Robert Thurman is Jey Tsong Khapa Professor of Indo-Tibetan Buddhist Studies, Chair of the Religion Department of Columbia University, and current President of Tibet House, an organization dedicated to the preservation of Tibetan culture. He is considered one of the leading American scholars of Tibetan Buddhism. He is also a lay Buddhist monk, and His Holiness the Fourteenth Dalai Lama, leader of the Tibetan Buddhist community in exile, considers him an old and trusted friend.*

Dr. Thurman graciously consented to read Ancient Secret of the Fountain of Youth, Book 1, *and consider the material it contains from both a historical and a spiritual perspective. He brought more than 30 years of practice and scholarship to our discussion. During the course of our conversation, he often referred to his own extensive writings on Tibet and Tibetan Buddhism, for he felt the questions we were exploring demanded much more background information than he could provide during our interview. With Dr. Thurman's permission, I have liberally interjected what I learned from reading his work into the text of this exchange.*

Question: What was your first reaction to *Ancient Secret of the Fountain of Youth* by Peter Kelder?

Robert Thurman: I found the book quite charming, with all the innocence of Hilton's *Lost Horizon*. Clearly it was written at a time when the Western view of Tibet was that it was a Shangri-La, a magical and remote paradise of possibilities. This view may have arisen from the very real fact that Tibet was a unique place in the world, the only country that put religion and spiritual advancement ahead of geopolitical and material advantage.

As Dr. Thurman's writings explain, up until the Chinese occupation of Tibet in 1950, when the systematic destruction of the country and its culture began, Tibet had evolved into a nation with a focus on self-conquest and spiritual accomplishment rather than military triumph. In the 17th century, the Fifth Dalai Lama was crowned King of Tibet, thus linking unequivocally the political and spiritual fate of the country. With virtually no interest in acquiring territory or power, the government funneled the wealth and energy of this small nation into the building of monasteries and the creation of religious art. Dedication to the principles of Tibetan Buddhism, not only in name but in practice, was public policy. Meditation was a national priority and spiritual adepts, or holy men, were the most valued members of the society.

One vivid expression of this commitment was The Great Prayer Festival of Lhasa, a national affirmation of spirituality, continuously observed for 551 years. For two weeks each year, all regular business was suspended and the keys of the city were symbolically turned over to the monks as the people of Tibet gathered together to pray and celebrate.

"The festival was a core event for all Tibet from 1409 until 1960," wrote Dr. Thurman, "when the Chinese occupation stopped it by force."

Q: Did this spirituality express itself in the ordinary interactions of the Tibetan people, in life as it was lived each day?

RT: This was a nonviolent culture and one that was rooted in attitudes of altruism, love, and compassion. In Tibetan Buddhism these concepts are promoted not only as religious ideals but as a way of life, a psychology of mind, and the teachings offer practical means to implement these principles. Imagine what it would be like for a Westerner, whose entire orientation is ego-centered and self-absorbed, to come upon such a peaceful culture, one that emphasized the happiness of others above all else and put that into practice in day-to-day life. That would indeed be Shangri-La.

Q: Could you talk more about the meaning of compassion within the context of Buddhist thought?

RT: You see and feel this compassionate presence in His Holiness the Dalai Lama. It is a very real thing, an energy and attention that extends itself from him to you. You can sense that he is not self-absorbed, that he cares more for you than for himself. And that is extraordinary when considered in the light of what he has suffered, what his country and his people have been through.

> I have found that the greatest degree of inner tranquillity comes from the development of love and compassion. The more we care for the happiness of others, the greater our own sense of well-being becomes. Thus we can strive gradually to become more compassionate, that is we can develop both genuine sympathy for others' suffering and the will to help remove their pain. As a result, our own serenity and inner strength will increase.
>
> Tenzin Gyatso, the Fourteenth Dalai Lama
> *Compassion and the Individual*

The Dalai Lama, age 14, during his flight from Tibet to India (1951), photographed by Heinrich Harrer. Harrer recalls, "On this occasion I took my final and best photo of the Fourteenth Dalai Lama; it was the very last photo made of His Holiness in free Tibet. I felt a deep anxiety about the young god-king, knowing that his country would soon be under the iron thumb of Mao Tse-tung."

Photograph by Heinrich Harrer

According to traditional Buddhist thinking, the practice of compassion, especially in the face of great obstacles, leads to a state of inner peace and well-being. That state has physical as well as mental benefits.

According to my personal experience, mental stability and physical well-being are directly related. Without question, anger and agitation make us more susceptible to illness. On the other hand, if the mind is tranquil and occupied with positive thoughts, the body will not easily fall prey to disease.

Tenzin Gyatso, the Fourteenth Dalai Lama
Compassion and the Individual

The relationship between physical health and mental stability described by the Dalai Lama is exactly what people who practice the Five Rites have experienced. They report improved health along with a definite decrease in tension and negative feelings, discovering a new sense of harmony between mind and body. This clearly relates to the ideas expressed by the Dalai Lama, and I asked Dr. Thurman how the rites fit in with the tenets of traditional Tibetan Buddhist beliefs.

Q: Could Colonel Bradford's story actually be true? Do you think the Five Rites, as they've been described for us in *Ancient Secret of the Fountain of Youth*, could have some real basis in Tibetan Buddhist practice as you understand it?
RT: The Five Rites strike me as reminiscent of Hatha yoga and seem to have more of the flavor of India than of Tibet. On the other hand, Buddhism was imported to Tibet from India some time in the 7th century A.D., and there is evidence that there was a great deal of scholarly exchange between the two countries. In the 8th century during the reign of the Emperor

Trisong Detsen, the first Tibetan monastery was built at Samye by an Indian Buddhist monk and Indian adept, and the best minds of India were invited to teach there. Tibetan Buddhism became the repository for much of the great and ancient teachings of India.

This might explain the fact that the Five Rites in *Fountain of Youth* appear to reflect yogic *tantras* (Buddhist and Hindu writings that combine practical religious instruction with physical disciplines).

Q: Could you expand on the relationship, as you see it, between the Five Rites and the principles of yoga?

RT: Shakyamuni, the historical Buddha, was himself a student of yoga. As Buddhism developed in Tibet, many Tibetans traveled to India to study, bringing back both yogic disciplines and sacred texts which they translated and incorporated into their own body of spiritual knowledge.

These rites likely spring from that knowledge base and so might give results similar to those achieved through yoga exercises, which come from an ancient physiologic tradition that has a proven beneficial effect on both the mind and the body.

There might also be a correspondence between the Hindu concept of *chakras*, the Buddhist idea of a subtle body comprised of what we might call energy fields, and the vortexes described in *Ancient Secret of the Fountain of Youth*. (See Chapter Four for further discussion of these ideas.)

According to Dr. Thurman, the Tantric yogas are literally technologies, precise methods for 'yoking,' or harnessing the life energies of the body to the quest for spiritual enlightenment through extraordinary physical efforts. In explaining the Buddhist science of physiology, Dr. Thurman has written that the subtle nervous system is a sensitive gyroscope-like structure of five or more 'wheels' within which energy and awareness circulate in a dynamic way. This description bears a close kinship to the spinning vortexes Peter Kelder describes.

Q: Are you surprised by the fact that the rites, which are purported to come from a very ancient tradition, seem to reflect a precise and rather advanced understanding of the body and how it works?

RT: The understanding of the mind and the body and the intricate relationship of the two evolved by the Tibetan Buddhists is unparalleled in any other tradition in the world. During the 9th century, hundreds of scholars from all over the world gathered in Tibet and spent a decade comparing the medical systems of India, China, Persia, Mongolia, and Uighuria. They created a unique medical system that integrated the best available psychology, anatomy, neurology, surgery, botany, chemistry, and nutrition with Buddhist spiritual technology. They developed very sophisticated healing arts, including methods, as I stated in *The Tibetan Book of the Dead*, for anticipating and warding off untimely death, and for prolonging human life.

"I believe," Dr. Thurman told another interviewer, "that the West will gradually come to recognize and appreciate these scientific and psychological principles that are part of the Buddhist tradition."

Q: Do you see a book like *Ancient Secret of the Fountain of Youth*, which presents some of those principles in a very simplified form, as a way to link East and West? In making the journey from one culture to another do you think the rites have weathered the trip intact? By that I mean, do they still seem to contain some of the intelligence that originally informed the vast and complex body of Tibetan Buddhist knowledge from which they supposedly originate?

RT: These rites are perhaps another way in which the wisdom of the East has made its way to the West. The story and the exercises are quite plausible and appear to possess some authenticity. The sixth rite of celibacy, for example, and the breathing that accompanies it is a very old and well-known concept, and the practice of it has long been associated with the youthful appearance often observed in Buddhist monks. From a scholarly point of view, I would say it's clear there was a real teacher who transmitted some legitimate information, information that can still be useful today.

Q: What chance would a modern-day seeker have of finding the kind of monastery Peter Kelder described? Does that Tibet still exist?

RT: Virtually all the monasteries in Tibet, a total of 6,250, have been ravaged since the Chinese invasion of Tibet in 1949. Tibetans have become a persecuted minority in their own country, forced to witness the devastation of their cities and their sacred places. It would not be extreme to say that Tibetans have experienced a holocaust at the hands of the invaders. Over a million people have been killed. Others who have fled to India live under the most difficult conditions. Though some monasteries have been rebuilt since the death of Mao, the propagation of Tibetan Buddhism is still illegal and the religious community in exile struggles to preserve and maintain their traditions and culture in the face of continuing oppression and destruction.

Q: What has become of the knowledge and traditions of Tibetan Buddhism, especially since 1959 when His Holiness the Fourteenth Dalai Lama was forced to flee his own country and take up residence in India?

RT: The attitude of Tibetan Buddhists towards the tremendous hardships they have faced since having to leave their country is that this adversity has helped them, sparking a profound renewal in faith and practice. Teachers are now traveling through both the Eastern and Western worlds, disseminating the great body of Tibetan knowledge as one means of preserving it.

> I must emphasize that merely thinking that compassion and reason and patience are good will not be enough to develop them. We must wait for difficulties to arise and attempt to practice them. And who creates such opportunities? Not our friends of course, but our enemies. They are the ones who give us the most trouble. So if we truly wish to learn, we should consider enemies to be our best teachers! For a person who cherishes compassion and love, the practice of tolerance is essential, and for that, an enemy is indispensable.

> Tenzin Gyatso, the Fourteenth Dalai Lama
> *Compassion and the Individual*

Q: You've said the Buddhist ideal is to develop oneself for the sake of others, and that spiritual progress depends upon a combination of ability and opportunity. Do you see a connection between Peter Kelder's account of a monastery where monks performed the Five Rites, which purportedly helped them live long and healthy lives, and the idea of opportunity?

RT: The foundation of Tibetan Buddhist thought is that each person desires true happiness for themselves but this happiness can be found only through the practice of compassion toward others. So you could say that Buddhist practice at its simplest level is about how to live a life infused with concern for the suffering of all others. The Buddhist monastic tradition represents a withdrawal from the world and all one's negative relationships in order to purify oneself in preparation for the practice of real compassion. Health and a long life certainly would enable one to do that better. I could see how the rites could have been part of an authentic teaching for Tibetan Buddhist monks, providing a means to a long, full life dedicated to compassionate action.

But it is important to understand that no true Tibetan Buddhist monastic community would have been practicing these rites as their main activity. They would have been part of a much larger, richer, deeper study and observance. A group of monks whose primary aim was to stay eternally young is peripheral to the goals and ideals of Tibetan Buddhist practice. But if the Five Rites are seen in the context of the Buddhist ideal that each person should strive to develop themselves to their highest potential for the sake of others, then there could be a philosophical basis for the emphasis on maintaining a vigorous and youthful state of health. To put it quite simply, we need to feel well in order to be able to help others, and enlightenment is not just a function of mind, but also includes the body.

The publisher and I would like to thank Dr. Robert Thurman and the staff of Tibet House in New York, an organization created by the current Dalai Lama, for their contributions to this volume. They have helped us to understand that the Five Tibetan Rites, as set down in Ancient Secret of the Fountain of Youth, *are only a small fragment of a much greater body of knowledge, and are part of a spiritual tradition that has survived the devastation of a country, a people, and a culture.*

Dr. Thurman dedicated his 1993 translation of The Tibetan Book of the Dead *to "...the brave and gentle people of Tibet, who have suffered and are suffering one of the great tragedies of our time.*

There is hope," he writes, "that the nations of the world, if they learn about Tibet in time, will not let the genocide of the six million Tibetans be completed in the 1990s."

If you are interested in contributing to Tibetan relief efforts, please turn to page 251 in the Afterword for information.

Laura Faye Taxel has been a writer, journalist, and researcher for more than 20 years. Her work has appeared in numerous national and local publications including Ladies Home Journal, Parenting, Natural Health, New Age, The Cleveland Plain Dealer Sunday Magazine, The Akron Beacon Journal Sunday Magazine and Cleveland Parent.

Laura is the author of Cleveland Ethnic Eats (Gray and Company, Inc., 1995), and she is currently working on several book projects on a variety of topics, including health and education.

PUBLISHER'S AFTERWORD

A strong sense of individualism is a hallmark of the Tibetan people, who have always fought hard to maintain their independence. For the last two thousand years, Tibet has recognized itself as a sovereign country with a long lineage of kings and lamas. Frequent Chinese and Mongol invasions threatened Tibet's independence, but the foreign invaders were usually defeated.

Then, between 1950 and 1959, the most devastating invasion of Tibet occurred. The Communist Chinese, inflamed by their Cultural Revolution, claimed Tibet as part of their "motherland." There was no historical or cultural basis for this, only military might.

The Chinese began systematically destroying Tibetan Buddhism across the land. Monasteries were ruined, monks and lamas murdered. Many of the ancient monasteries were literally blown up by dynamite or mortar shell. The roofs of hermitages were removed so that they would be quickly destroyed by the elements. Invaluable spiritual texts were burned or used as toilet paper. Libraries were ransacked. Religious objects were turned into rubble. Once venerated temples were used as pigsties and slaughterhouses. Sacred clay images were stamped into dust or made into building bricks. Of the approximately 600,000 monks living in Tibet before the Chinese invasion, only an estimated 7,000 survived; as many as 100,000 fled the country. Within three years of the Chinese invasion, Tibet was scarred by ruins, resembling the bombed cities of Europe after World War II.

Perhaps even worse, China introduced an estimated seven million Han Chinese into Tibet, making native Tibetans a minority in their own country.

Some characterize this desecration of Tibet as the Buddhist Holocaust. Since the invasion of Tibet, an estimated 1.2 million Tibetans have died, victims of violence, execution, imprisonment, torture, starvation, and suicide. Thousands more have fled Tibet. They struggle to survive in refugee settlements under conditions of extreme poverty and deprivation.

Tibet and Tibetan Buddhism Today

Today, hundreds of Tibetans are being held as political prisoners in one of Lhasa's four jails. The situation now resembles the mood of Eastern Europe during the Communist era. There are numerous Chinese spies and informers in Tibet, free speech is non-existent, and many Tibetans live in fear and desperation. As of the mid-1990s, Tibet is the world's longest (and largest) occupied sovereign state.

For many in the West, Tibet's spiritual and political leader, the Fourteenth Dalai Lama, is the face of that shattered and struggling nation. In 1959, he was persuaded to flee to Dharamsala, India where he established and still maintains a government-in-exile. In spite of the atrocities committed by the Chinese, he believes that the cultivation of compassion and non-violent diplomacy is the only route to world peace and the only path for the Tibetan people. The recipient of the 1989 Nobel Peace Prize, he recently told a reporter for the *New York Times* that "the Tibetan resistance has worldwide support because it is non-violent." He also said that he is hopeful for the eventual restitution of the Tibetan homeland. In his autobiography he wrote, "Thus, despite the continuing tragedy of Tibet, I find much good in the world."

There are a number of non-profit organizations dedicated to advancing the Tibetan cause. If you would like to find out how you can help, please contact the following:

TIBET HOUSE
22 West 15th Street
New York, NY 10111
Tel: 212-213-5592
Fax: 212-213-6408

Tibet House is devoted to efforts to save Tibetan culture from the threat of extinction. The Tibet House Cultural Center in midtown Manhattan hosts exhibits and cultural events, and its Tibetan Studies Program offers classes in Tibetan language, art, history, medicine, and spiritual sciences. Tibet House also maintains an archive of old Tibetan photographs and a program to conserve art and artifacts.

THE TIBET FUND
241 East 32nd Street
New York, NY 10016
Tel: 212-213-5011
Fax: 212-779-9245

The Tibet Fund addresses the needs of the Tibetan refugee community in India, Nepal, and elsewhere. The Tibet Fund's primary mission is to help support and strengthen this community through programs in education, health, economic and community development, and religion. A donor may sponsor a monk or nun at a monastic institution, or a child at a refugee school.

TIBETAN RIGHTS CAMPAIGN
P.O. Box 31966
Seattle, WA 98103-0066
Tel: 206-547-1015,
Fax: 206-547-3758

The Tibetan Rights Campaign (TRC) works to raise awareness of the plight of the Tibetan people and to advance their struggle for human rights, democracy, and independence. Their work includes cultural events; talks, videos, and slide shows; *Tibet Monitor*, a monthly news report on developments concerning Tibet; a lending library of books on Tibet; and quarterly membership meetings.

INTERNATIONAL CAMPAIGN FOR TIBET
1825 K Street NW, Suite 520
Washington, DC 20006
Tel: 202-785-1515
Fax: 202-785-4343

The International Campaign for Tibet (ICT) is a nonpartisan, public interest group dedicated to promoting human rights and democratic freedoms for the people of Tibet. ICT believes that governments and people around the world need accurate information on current conditions in Tibet.

A P P E N D I X   A

How to Organize Your Own Himalaya Club

The Himalaya Club was a group led by Colonel Bradford that met regularly to practice the Five Rites and discuss related matters such as diet and nutrition (see Chapters One and Six).

If you're interested in organizing your own Himalaya Club, here are a few suggestions to get you started:

1. Place an advertisement in a local newspaper, magazine, or newsletter. Here's a sample:

   Do you want to discover how much energy you have inside? Would you like to feel and look years younger and healthier? Meet regularly to practice and discuss five simple, effective exercises that can change your life. You'll be amazed. Write...

2. Introduce your friends, relatives, and co-workers to the Five Rites and Peter Kelder's *Ancient Secret of the Fountain of Youth, Book 1,* by lending them a copy of the book or buying books as gifts. After seeing the remarkable results you have experienced, the people in your life will probably want to join your group.

3. Contact local yoga teachers and yoga groups to see if they

253

can recommend ways to get in touch with yoga practitioners who might be interested in participating in a Himalaya Club.

4. Lead a discussion group on *Ancient Secret of the Fountain of Youth, Book 1*, in your home, local libraries, community centers, or places of worship. Be sure to have a sign-in sheet at the front of the room so you can contact attendees later.

5. Put up notices on bulletin boards in health food stores, health clubs, gyms, yoga centers, community centers, etc. using an advertisement similar to the one provided above in suggestion #1.

Anyone can organize a Himalaya Club. All you need is a group of interested participants.

A P P E N D I X   B

Healing Experiences of People Who Practice the Five Rites

by Laura Faye Taxel

In this appendix you will meet people I spoke with at length about their experiences with the Five Rites. While each person has a different story to tell, the end results are all the same: The Five Rites produce renewed health, vitality, energy, and a sense of well-being in the people who practice them regularly.

Past Seventy and Too Young to Slow Down

When physical therapist Suzanne Barnes took her 72-year-old mother, Henrietta Slater, to Toronto as a Christmas present, a typical day for both of them included a workout in the hotel's fitness center plus seven or eight miles of walking around the city as sightseers. Mrs. Slater has been doing the Five Rites for two-and-a-half years, ever since her daughter gave her a copy of *Ancient Secret of the Fountain of Youth*, and she's a perfect example of the many ways the Five Rites can enrich the quality of life for those who practice them.

"I was so impressed with the results I experienced from doing the Five Rites," said Mrs. Slater of Dubuque, Iowa, "that

I bought copies for my other eight children, plus friends. I am a health education coordinator at a rural health center and I demonstrate the Five Rites in my weight reduction series as a good form of exercise for a healthy lifestyle."

Henrietta Slater is at an age when most people find themselves slowing down, whether they want to or not, but not Netta, as her friends call her. She keeps very busy with her job at a local clinic, a ten room home, church, and community activities. "I just seem to be energized since I added these rites to my life," she says. "I had a back injury fifteen years ago, and my daughter Suzanne gave me some warm-up exercises, but by themselves they didn't do anything like what the rites do for me. I've begun to feel like I'm getting younger. I'm happy with the way I look, and more important, I'm happy with the way I feel. I work four days a week doing nutritional counseling and educational programs about healthy living and wellness for senior citizens, and even though I'm the same age as my audiences, I don't feel like one of them."

Mrs. Slater, who's a trim 5'6" and 122 pounds is awake at 5:00 a.m. every morning. She begins her day by meditating, then performs the Five Rites, and finds herself so full of vim and vigor that she's ready to take her dog for a mile walk through the woods behind her house, no matter what the weather. She and the dog walk another mile in the evening. At the health center where she works, she's often around people who are ill but for the past couple of years she hasn't gotten sick even once, and didn't get a flu shot either. Her back no longer gives her any discomfort, and best of all she shows no signs of developing the arthritis that runs in her family. "I'm convinced the Five Rites are what's helping me," says Mrs. Slater. "By practicing them daily I seem to be avoiding the problems of aging. It takes real discipline to actually do them, but because I am doing them every day, I'm enjoying the benefits."

Dan Hanville, 76, gives his wife, Helen, who insisted he do the Five Rites along with her, all the credit for their lives getting easier and better. "I was skeptical at first and started doing the rites only because it meant so much to Helen," said Dan. "She fumed and fussed at me to do them, and do them right. After six months, I told her that I was doing them for myself because I could really see a difference in how I felt—no more arthritis aches and pains, more energy, and most of all, our friends started to say that I was looking so much younger. One person told me I didn't look any different than when he'd last seen me five years ago."

"I can't even begin to describe to you how this has changed our lives," said Helen, who is 68 years old. "Neither one of us has any of the pain or stiffness we were used to having. I've gotten back the figure I had when I was 18. People have always described me as a fireball but what I love is that I'm not slowing down now. I have much more energy than I had before and it's clear to me that we both have a new sense of well-being. It's physical and emotional. It makes Dan very happy when people tell him how good he looks. I notice he walks differently than he used to. There's more spring in his step. I think we both look younger to people because we act younger. And we act younger because we feel so much better. I just know we're going to keep on following the advice in *Ancient Secret of the Fountain of Youth* until we die. We don't so much want to live long as live healthy."

"And the rites," added Dan, "are what has made the difference in our lives, a tremendous difference."

George and Lynell Roberts, both 60 years old, live in a little house in the hills of western Oregon. George works full time in a management position for a large manufacturing company. Lynell, retired from her job with the Humane Society, still seems to attract every stray bird, dog, and cat in the county. These days she has a great deal of work to do caring for the animals, keeping their acre of grass mowed, and tending a small vegetable garden. But neither Lynell nor her husband enjoyed their lives before they discovered the Five Rites. Lynell suffered a crippling stroke in 1988 that left her unable to walk without a cane. She also had severe arthritis in her knees, and she often fell. Sometimes, at night, the pain in her legs would be so bad she couldn't sleep. She had chronic sinus problems that regularly turned into sinus infections. She had a smoker's cough and was overweight. George had quadruple bypass heart surgery in 1984. He continued to have congestive heart troubles and was diabetic.

Their daughter, worried about them, convinced Lynell to get *Ancient Secret of the Fountain of Youth* after seeing an advertisement for the book. "After all," she told her mother, "at that price, anything is worth a try." The book arrived the same day George came home from his latest stay in the hospital. He read it cover to cover and the couple began the exercises immediately, both able to do only three or four repetitions of each rite. Later that same week, George went to his doctor who expressed concern about a "tick" he heard in George's heart.

The couple added the Five Rites to their daily routine. It was the only regular exercise either one did. At George's follow-up visit to his doctor, the "tick" was gone, and at his most recent check-up, the doctor told George that his heart sounded good and his arteries were in excellent shape for someone with his condition. He also told George that although many people often require a second surgery after ten years, he did not.

Lynell, too, had begun to notice improvements in her health. She found that she was able to get down on the floor and back up again without help. Her sinus problems disappeared and the chronic sinus infections she was prone to, have not recurred. Her breathing improved and she noticed that she hardly coughed anymore. She lost ten pounds within the first two months, and another five pounds in the following months. She was able to walk normally, though still slowly, and no longer fell. If arthritis pain made her uncomfortable at night, she could alleviate it by getting up and doing a few repetitions of each rite.

The Five Rites have become an essential part of Lynell and George's life, and Lynell calls them a godsend. "We've never stayed with any other form of exercise," said Lynell, "and believe me, we've tried. We've had a rowing machine, a treadmill. But I think the rites are about more than just the body. They put your mind into focus, too. I know, for me, they worked on my mood, my mental state. That was proven to me when my son died in April, 1994. I fell into a deep depression and stopped doing almost everything including the Five Rites. It almost destroyed me. But then I started to do the rites again and something changed. My energy began to pick up, my thinking was clearer, and I suddenly had the will to survive. I got my physical and emotional balance back, and each day after I do them, I feel strong enough to handle things in my life.

"I believe those Tibetan monks discovered something we all need," Lynell continued. "They learned how to take care of themselves and I'm glad their secret is out now. It's helped me to realize that George and I don't have to grow ill and feeble as we grow older."

Physical and Emotional Balance

For Nancy Brown the changes brought about by the Five Rites were emotional and physical in equal measure and, according to Nancy, she was in desperate need of help in both areas of her life. After having worked for the same company for over 20 years, she was terminated in 1991, at age 62. It was a devastating blow to Nancy's self-esteem as well as her lifestyle, which, as a divorced woman with grown children, had come to revolve primarily around her career.

"When I was let go, I became very depressed and my asthma, which I've had since I was three years old got very bad, triggered by all the stress and tension," explained Nancy. "I could hardly walk without getting out of breath."

Nancy's asthma and depression seemed to feed off each other, and she grew reclusive, reluctant to leave her apartment or even answer the telephone. She was put on heavy doses of medication that included a nasal spray, three inhalers to be used four times a day, and oral Prednisone, a steroid that made her weight jump up by 35 pounds. Another side effect of steroids is that they may weaken joint cartilage, and the medication Nancy was taking caused her to have problems in her hips and legs.

Then she heard about *Ancient Secret of the Fountain of Youth*. Always interested in anything related to health, Nancy bought the book, read it, and knowing she was in the midst of a real health crisis of her own, started doing the Five Rites.

"I could barely do three of each at first, but I kept trying, building up the number of repetitions because I began to feel better right away," said Nancy. "It really worked for me. As my body began to feel better, I felt better about myself. I began to go out, and realized that people were glad to see me. The stronger I felt, the less depressed I became."

Nancy hasn't had a full-blown asthma attack or been to the

emergency room for treatment in the two years that she's been doing the Five Rites, although both were all too common before. Even better, she was able to stop taking almost all of her medications. Now she takes no steroids at all, and only needs a single inhaler occasionally when humidity and allergens are at their peak in Mount Kisco, New York, where she lives. And she's found a rewarding new career volunteering as a foster grandparent for special-needs children.

Nancy had another long-standing problem before she began doing the Five Rites. She had hurt her back, spraining the upper half during a severe coughing bout caused by an attack of bronchial asthma, and injuring the lower portion in a fall down a flight of steps. Weekly visits to a chiropractor kept her discomfort at a tolerable level, though she said that many mornings she was so stiff and sore she could only get out of bed by rolling out onto the floor. "I don't need to see the chiropractor anymore," says Nancy, "and if I'm a little stiff when I wake up, I immediately do my Five Rites and I feel fine for the rest of the day. I can move easily and comfortably and keep up with the three- and four-year-old children I work with." Nancy, a 5'2" blonde, is also back to her normal weight of 120.

A few weeks after interviewing Nancy I received the following letter from her:

Dear Laura,

Since speaking with you, I have continued to think about the Five Rites and wanted to tell you how I know they are really working for me.

At one time, I wondered if it was all just in my mind because I wanted to believe they could help. Then I started participating in the Foster Grandparent Program. I loved working with the children, but found it very tiring. So instead of doing the Five Rites every morning as I had been, I decided to sleep for the extra half-hour.

Within a week, the pain in my back returned and I started to feel depressed. I had problems with my asthma and had to increase my medication. I was angry with almost everything and everybody, except the children I worked with and my family. I hid it quite well and no one noticed, but I could feel it inside me.

One morning, I got up half an hour earlier and did the Five Rites. My back felt much better. I continued this routine. One week later my asthma was under control and two weeks later I was able to cut back on my medication. Instead of depression, I had good feelings about myself, life, and everything around me. I felt elated and peaceful.

I will never again miss a day of doing the Five Rites. I have proven to myself that they do work for me.

Sincerely,
Nancy

A Cure for Arthritis and a New Lease on Life

The Five Rites certainly worked for Gladys Rogan. At 62, four years younger than Nancy, Gladys was bone tired and ready to retire. She had arthritis in her knees that caused excruciating pain, especially at night, and she often walked with a limp. Her blood pressure, her cholesterol, and her blood sugar were one step away from being on the wrong side of the doctor's balance sheet. Her aging mother had begun to need a lot of care and Gladys didn't know where she'd find the energy to tend to her.

A friend gave her a copy of *Ancient Secret of the Fountain of Youth* but Gladys put it aside, unopened. When she came upon the book some months later, she took it with her to read on the subway going to work in a midtown Manhattan department store. Thinking things couldn't get worse than they already were, she decided to give these strange Tibetan exercises a try. Seven weeks later, she felt like a new person.

"I had lunch with the friend who'd sent me the book and she told me I glowed," said Gladys proudly. "Said I looked like I'd dropped 20 years since she last saw me. In the past two years since I've been doing the rites, my arthritis has just about disappeared. Used to be I had to take painkillers just to get through the night and slept with a pillow tucked under my knees. But no more. I sleep fine, I walk fine, and never need to wrap my knees in elastic bandages the way I used to. I don't need any medicine. My cholesterol, my blood sugar, and my pressure are all normal. I can hardly believe it. I know it sounds too good to be true, but it is true."

Even though she got her health back, Gladys decided to retire as she'd planned. But instead of resting, she's busier than ever. She travels by subway across town to see her mother every day, and tutors two days a week at a local public school. "I feel like my retirement turned into a whole new life for me," said Gladys. "I do everything I want to and have no health problems. I know now that you don't have to get old as long as you feel young. I told my friend Mabel, who gave me the book, that when I get to be 90 like my mother, I expect to be in great shape. And by the way, you should see Mabel. She's 62, and since she started doing these rites she positively bubbles. She's taking singing lessons, too. The book is our bible."

The Power of Perseverance

Jerry Henderson, 61, of Oakbrook, Illinois, did the rites for two years, felt great, and then began to slack off, doing them only occasionally. Old problems resurfaced, but he didn't make the connection until he had a conversation with an old friend who asked for suggestions about how to get in shape. Jerry remembered how much the Five Rites had helped him, gave his friend a copy of the book, and reread it himself. That was almost two years ago. Since then, he says he's been doing the rites "religiously."

Jerry was a serious athlete in his youth. He played football, excelled at tennis, and was a Big Ten discus champion in college. But all that took a toll on his body and over the years he needed two operations on his shoulder, and had chronic pain in his lower back, his left knee, his right Achilles tendon, and his wrist. When he moved to California, the land of the physically fit and the eternally young, being able to remain active seemed more important than ever. Now that he understands how much the Five Rites contribute to that ability, he's never going to stop again. He thinks the rites not only help him keep fit but also keep him focused on what's important. They're a sort of daily touchstone for health.

"What they've given me carries over into all the rest of my life. I feel good about myself and I've become a believer," he said. "The effects may be difficult to measure but in my case the evidence is overwhelming. Since I resumed the daily practice of the rites, I no longer have any pain in my back, my shoulder, my wrist, my knee, or my Achilles. I can bench press 120 pounds, 20 times, and I've found the rites are terrific as a warm-up for weight lifting. I play tennis four or five times a week with players who are ranked among the best in the state and I can hold my own. In fact, my game's improving. I'm very quick on my feet. My scores, which compare favorably with theirs, give me a good indication of what great shape I'm in. I used to have high blood pressure but it is perfectly normal now. I just took an insurance exam and passed for preferred coverage. The doctor commented that I had the heart of an athlete."

Jerry finds the rites useful for relieving stress and body tension, too. When he has trouble falling asleep, he'll get out of bed, spend ten minutes doing the Five Rites and then, totally relaxed, is able to fall asleep immediately.

Because Jerry had the experience of doing the rites, then stopping and starting again, he speaks with authority when he says, "The key to success is to do them regularly, be patient about results, and then miracles can happen. But it takes time. Once you've decided to do them, you have to stay with it and believe that they can help you. And they will."

APPENDIX C

Hatha Traditions: How to Find a Class That's Right for You

by Linda Johnsen

You want to take a Hatha class. You've heard that Hatha limbers, relaxes, and strengthens the body, while toning the internal organs and stimulating the endocrine glands—and you're ready to give it a try. Or maybe you took a few classes some years ago and miss the motivation and support a regular class provides. So you open a yoga directory to find out where the nearest courses are being taught.

If you're like me, you may find yourself staring at the pages of class offerings in bewilderment. I thumbed through a lengthy list of local classes and found some teachers credentialed by Integral Yoga International, some certified as Iyengar practitioners, and other instructors noting their kundalini yoga training. What does it all mean? Are these classes more or less the same or is there some dramatic difference that I should know about before I sign up?

I started feeling a little anxious as I pored over the teachers' credentials. I'd heard rumors about instructors stomping on their students' backs while the students lay in the crocodile pose, and although I am sure there are people who benefit from this method of teaching, I suspect I wouldn't be one. I want to make sure the Hatha course I sign up for is one I'll feel comfortable in — that the teacher and I are thinking along pretty much the same lines in terms of what we hope to give to and get from a Hatha yoga session.

Then I noticed that although there are a lot of teachers out there, the number of lineages they represent is surprisingly few. Discover who the founder of a particular Hatha tradition is and you've got an important clue to the type of Hatha being taught. The late Swami Sivananda, the prolific sage from Rishikesh, authored dozens of books on many aspects of yoga and fostered at least four major branches of American Hatha yoga. He was the guru of Swami Satchidananda and of Swami Vishnu-devananda. Vishnu-devananda's disciple Yogi Hari comes from this lineage, as does television's best-known Hatha teacher, Lilias Folan.

Krishnamacharya, head of the Yoga Institute at the royal palace of Mysore, had a big effect on the development of contemporary Hatha. He was B. K. S. Iyengar's teacher, and also taught K. Pattabhi Jois, who was in turn the teacher of Hatha's other great television proselytizer, Richard Freeman. The Hatha master Desikachar, enormously popular in Europe, is also from this tradition.

Other teachers from India who dramatically influenced the way Hatha is taught in this country include Paramahansa Yogananda, Swami Rama, Swami Kripalvananda, and Yogi Bhajan. I decided to approach representatives from these major traditions to ask exactly what you and I can expect when we sign up for a Hatha yoga course with one of their certified instructors.

Iyengar

B. K. S. Iyengar's leonine figure looms over the development of Hatha yoga in the twentieth century. Since he first came to the United States in 1974, his precise style of working with the asanas and detailed attention to alignment have made him one of the world's most respected Hatha authorities.

I asked Janet MacLeod, who has been teaching in this tradition for fifteen years, if it's true the Iyengar style is the most vigorous form of Hatha being practiced today. "There's a whole range of classes, varying from the easier, restorative classes all the way up to doing jumping in the sun salute," she answered. "On the whole it is a little more rajasic (dynamic) than some of the other styles. I'm not sure if it's so much vigorous as it is just demanding mentally, because we pay a lot of attention to detail.

"We're not necessarily holding the poses longer. In fact Mr. Iyengar advises beginning students not to hold them very long at all. It's better to do the pose several times for a shorter period in the beginning so that the student doesn't develop any unnecessary tension struggling to do the pose. You don't have to be an athlete to do Iyengar yoga. Mr. Iyengar has the skill to tailor a posture to all kinds of different bodies, from somebody who can't even walk into the Institute to somebody who's quite an advanced student.

"In the beginning we emphasize standing postures. This teaches people to align their bodies and balance on their feet, so when they come to do inverted positions they already have a high degree of sensitivity.

"If people can't touch the floor or can't get the proper alignment or lift in a pose, we use blocks and belts and bolsters and blankets. Maintaining the correct spinal alignment is difficult if the shoulders and hips are tight, so we make accommodation for that by using the props. That way people who aren't strong can benefit from a pose and can stay in the posture without using physical effort at all.

"The greatest strength of Iyengar yoga is that the quality of teacher education is very high. Our training program takes a minimum of two years. Most people don't pass in two years; they take four or five years. The course, taught here in San Francisco and perhaps soon in New York and Los Angeles as well, covers anatomy, physiology, kinesiology, and yoga philosophy, as well as all the more up-to-date techniques of teacher training and student/teacher relationships. The training is quite professional, very much like going to college."

You can reach the Iyengar Yoga Institute of San Francisco at 415-753-0909 to ask for more information.

Kripalvananda

Next I spoke with Devakanya G. Parnell, Director of Resident Yoga Education at the Kripalu Center in Lenox, Massachusetts. Although Kripalu was founded by Amrit Desai, the inspiration for Kripalu's yoga program came originally from Kripalvananda, an Indian master of kundalini yoga whose primary practice was actually pranayama (breath control). Devakanya catches me completely off-guard when she comments, "A lot of the postures taught in India are not really appropriate for Western bodies. The kind of bodies that can do the kundalini postures are usually thin, with little bulk and long limbs. Unless you have that kind of body those postures are very, very difficult. What we have developed here at Kripalu is more in tune with the Western body and temperament and is more in accord with Western psychological theories." Remembering how I used to struggle with postures that required arms six inches longer and twice as strong as mine, I find myself listening to her views with sympathy.

"There are three stages to Kripalu yoga," Devakanya explains. "In Stage One, willful practice, you learn to pay precise attention to the alignment and details of the posture and how to breathe deeply, coordinating breath with movement." Postures are held for ten or twenty seconds. "Benefits come, not from maximum strength or flexibility, but from holding the correct form of the posture. Accepting and honoring the limitations of your body rather than fighting them.

"Stage Two, will and surrender, involves prolonged holding. In this stage you learn to withdraw your outgoing, scattered attention (*pratyahara* sense control) and focus it inward, anchoring it in bodily sensations (*dharana* concentration). When you prolong the holding, you enter into the field of unconscious fears and resistances. Maintain an unbroken stream of attention, acknowledging and flowing with the changing emotions that arise. When you come to your toleration point during prolonged holding, you encounter your self-perceived limitations and learn how to consciously transcend them." This is a valuable lesson, Devakanya tells us, that applies to dealing with one's emotional reactions during daily life.

Stage Three is surrender to the wisdom of the body. Here the postures are allowed to emerge spontaneously, guided by the body's own inner knowing. Traditional postures or wholly new ways of holding and moving the body may appear by themselves. "Done in this way yoga postures become a form of meditation in motion, a prayer without words. The unobstructed flow of prana (life energy) guides the body."

Kripalu offers a full range of intensity — gentle, moderate, and vigorous — within each of the three stages. As Devakanya speaks, the combination of Kripalvananda's original emphasis on working with prana and modern Western psychological insights becomes apparent. "Within the body is a subtle flow of rhythmic energy pulsations. Even the most insignificant thought can disturb or block this flow. But as you dissolve mental and emotional disturbance through practice, tremendous amounts of prana are released. That life energy spontaneously retards the aging process; it strengthens and rejuvenates all the systems of the body. Thus you progressively accelerate those internal healing processes that enable you to awaken to the higher centers of consciousness."

While the Kripalu community is based in Lenox, the Kripalu Yoga Teachers' Association is a worldwide network of certified teachers practicing in this tradition. For more information call 800-967-3577 and ask for Kyta.

Paramhansa Yogananda

Yogananda? Most of us don't usually associate the much-loved North Indian teacher—whose classic book Autobiography of a Yogi has been turning people on to meditation for half a century now—with Hatha yoga. Yet the program "Yoga Postures for Higher Awareness" taught at the Ananda community in Nevada City, California, is a direct outgrowth of Yogananda's work.

I spoke with Savitri, a resident at Ananda for eighteen years and Director of the Teacher Training Program. She explained, "Yogananda didn't really emphasize Hatha yoga. When he was giving talks back in the 1920s and 1930s he would sometimes have his students demonstrate the postures, but it was not a central part of his teaching."

One of Yogananda's direct disciples, however, was fascinated by aspects of Hatha yoga the master had taught and decided to expand them into a fourteen-step system. The disciple—J. Donald Walters, founder of Ananda—kept in mind Yogananda's teaching that the true purpose of yoga is to prepare the student for the experience of self-realization.

Walters' system of yoga "teaches the postures in all their physical aspects but goes into the more spiritual aspects of each one also, and adds certain things like doing an affirmation in your mind while you're doing a stretch with your body," Savitri says. In this way you develop a new enlightened relationship with your body.

The system also includes Yogananda's unique Energization Exercises. "They're a series of exercises that Yogananda developed in 1917, when he first founded the Ranchi School for Boys in India. He would have them do a short calisthenics set — except that instead of just jumping around he taught the boys to mentally direct energy to different parts of the body as they were moving. These exercises take about fifteen minutes to do once you learn them. They're quite subtle; they involve tensing and relaxing different parts of the body, consciously sending energy through the different body parts, and using certain breathing exercises that go along with tensing and relaxing. Some of them increase the heart rate, and some of them work on the polarity in the brain. They were way ahead of their time."

How hard is it to do the postures taught at Ananda? "Our program is definitely on the gentle side, the reason being that we're doing the yoga postures with a meditative attitude, in preparation for meditation itself.

"One of the strengths of our program is that it's geared to the spiritual; for people who are cultivating the spiritual dimensions of their life, that's really nice. The other strength is that it is a whole yoga community; it's not just a place where you go and take classes. There are 300 people living here, and everyone meditates, so you get that really strong spiritual environment around you. You almost learn by osmosis."

Hatha classes, as well as Ananda's month-long Teacher Training Program, are offered at the Expanding Light facility in Nevada City, and at Ananda's branch communities in Sacramento, Portland, and Assisi (Italy). The series "Yoga Postures for Higher Awareness" is also taught at Ananda's communities in Palo Alto, Seattle, and Dallas. Call 800-346-5350 for more information about Ananda's style of yoga.

Swami Rama

Swami Rama exploded Western scientific myths about the limitations of human physiology when, in 1970, researchers at the Menninger Foundation in Topeka, Kansas, discovered that the yogi from North India could control his autonomic nervous system—which any well-trained physician knew was impossible. Swami Rama virtually stopped his heart for extended periods of time, remained fully lucid while his brain registered the delta waves normally associated with deep sleep, and otherwise confounded astonished researchers. Anyone who had previously discounted yogis as a bunch of eccentrics standing on their heads was rudely awakened: clearly there was more to yoga than most people in the West had suspected.

I spoke with Shirley Walter, head of the Himalayan Institute Teachers' Association, about how her experiences with Swami Rama in the 1970s have influenced Hatha training at the Himalayan Institute today.

"Swamiji taught Hatha as part of a complete and systematic path for introducing students to their inner selves. It's not just a set of difficult physical exercises for the athletically inclined. It's really training the mind through the body.

"Body awareness leads us to the higher awareness of the subtle energy [prana] as well as the thinking process, and finally we are aware of the functioning of the nervous system and become very sensitive to the sleeping part of the brain—the unconscious. So Hatha is preparation for control and direction of the meditative experience.

"We start people wherever they are. If they're very stiff and out of shape, sick, or weak, we have a whole set of exercises to loosen the joints and stimulate circulation as well as work with the glands, which control our health and the proper functioning of the body. If practiced regularly these simple exercises alone make an enormous difference in a person's health and well-being.

"Other students may go right into practicing the asanas. Although we teach several levels of Hatha classes, we address varying levels of ability within the same class by introducing modifications and preparations as individual needs dictate. Every class has a similar structure designed to derive maximum benefit from the postures, and all the major groups of postures are covered in a single class. Always we emphasize inner awareness and mind-body coordination. The breath is the means for achieving that awareness, and it is the link to the mind and the more subtle aspects of being. We emphasize the breathing practices more than most schools of Hatha — our students learn a very systematic method of working with the breath as well as understanding the dynamics of the breathing process. We also emphasize relaxation techniques.

"In our system, you first work with the asanas to purify, align, and strengthen the body; then you practice a deep systematic relaxation to release all tension; finally you use the breath to draw the mind and senses inward and move on to the other rungs on the eight-step ladder of raja yoga. These are the keys to unlocking the secret wealth in the body. Our Hatha yoga system is designed to keep the body in good shape, but in truth, in its advanced stages, this system is actually the gateway to the subtle body — the safest, easiest, and surest way to discover the mysteries of the human body, psyche, and soul."

The Himalayan Institute yoga-meditation programs are available throughout the country. For more information about the Himalayan Institute and its branches, call 800-822-4547. To locate an accredited teacher in your area, call 708-724-0300.

Swami Satchidananda

The great master of Rishikesh, Swami Sivananda, taught a synthesis of many different types of yoga. His disciples—including such renowned swamis as Satchidananda, Chidananda (the late President of the Divine Life Society), Jyotirmayananda, and the late Vishnu-devananda—would carry this synthesis to all parts of the world.

Swami Satchidananda won himself a permanent place in the hearts of Baby Boomers when he presided as spiritual mentor at Woodstock in 1969, and taught an entire generation to chant "Om." His lavishly illustrated book Integral Yoga Hatha was the bible for thousands of aspiring American yogis in the early 1970s.

Swami Karunananda, President of the Yogaville Ashram in Buckingham, Virginia, spoke with me about the practice of Satchidananda's Integral Yoga in the 1990s. "Hatha yoga is the doorway through which most people enter. Most people face problems with stress and fatigue, and come to learn to relax and increase their vitality. They start there, then get more interested in the underlying principles of yoga. For us, Hatha yoga is the way to get the body fit, while meditation is the way to make the mind focused, calm, and clear. Both are meant to prepare the body and mind for a useful, dedicated life. Satchidananda uses the words easeful, peaceful, and useful: the body should be easeful, the mind should be peaceful, and the life should be useful.

"Some schools advise spending many hours a day doing Hatha. We advise that thirty minutes of Hatha a day, followed by another half hour of pranayama and meditation, is sufficient to help keep the physical mechanism in good repair to meet life's challenges. Hatha is a means, not an end.

"Our approach is gentle, meditative. Hatha is a meditation for the body. It works on the nervous and endocrine systems. Our classes are scientifically designed to gently bring you toward an inward focus as you meditate on the motion of the physical body. After forty minutes of asanas we do a deep relaxation, letting the energy flow freely, and then we do pranayama, working with the pranic body. We do rapid breathing to energize and awaken the system, then alternate nostril breathing to balance and calm the system. This helps get the mind in the optimal state to enter more deeply within. Finally we have a brief period of meditation, working with the mental body. Ultimately both physical and mental experiences are transcended; we experience the truth behind them.

"Integral Yoga is based on the natural spiritual awakening of the kundalini force through gradual purification of the physical and mental levels. We don't use more vigorous methods — we go the slow, safe route.

"A body of perfect health and strength, mind with all clarity and calmness, intellect as sharp as a razor, will as pliable as steel, heart full of love and compassion, life full of dedication, and realization of the true Self is the goal of Integral Yoga," Swami Satchidananda wrote 25 years ago when he first introduced Americans to his system of yoga. Its goal has not changed.

For more information about Integral Yoga, call 800-858-YOGA.

Swami Vishnu-devananda

Vishnu-devananda catapulted to fame in the West with the publication of *The Complete Illustrated Book of Yoga* in 1960, a book that has inspired thousands of determined Western yogis to master the believable postures Vishnu-devananda demonstrated.

Srinivasan, Director of the Sivananda Ashram Yoga Ranch in Woodbourne, New York, explained to me how Hatha is taught today at the numerous centers founded by Swami Vishnu-devananda. "Swamiji introduced Hatha yoga in the West as five points: follow proper exercise (asanas) to stretch and strengthen the muscular system and stimulate circulation; proper breathing (pranayama) to recharge and balance one's nervous and subtle pranic systems; proper relaxation (shavasana) to cool down the muscles, breath, and mind; proper diet (vegetarian), teaching self-discipline in diet and consumption; positive thinking (Vedanta philosophy) and meditation (dhyana), identification with the immortal soul. For the beginner, Hatha yoga offers a practical method for disciplining one's life in order to cultivate health, peace of mind, and happiness. For more serious practitioners, though, the asanas and pranayama, along with the ethical disciplines of yama and niyama, form the foundation of raja yoga, which is the yoga of self-realization through meditation and mastery of one's mind.

"Sivananda Hatha yoga classes are highly structured, based on a routine of breathing exercises, sun salutations, a series of twelve classic yoga postures, and relaxation. Classes begin and end with a short mantra chant and prayers. We encourage students to deepen their yoga practice with meditation, devotional practices, and Vedanta, but these are taught in separate courses or at our ashrams, where guests participate in a full daily routine incorporating all the major yoga disciplines."

What will a student find when he or she first walks into a Sivananda Hatha class? "A new student can expect excellent, balanced, authentic yoga classes from Sivananda teachers, which can become either a cornerstone of a new, healthier lifestyle or a foundation for a complete spiritual practice," Srinivasan replied. "We encourage students to go slowly, but to develop a definite routine. We offer a very firm foundation in our beginner's courses, and because our teachers take yoga as a complete lifestyle, serious students can expect to be guided as far down the path of Hatha and raja yoga as they can commit themselves to the disciplined practice."

The Sivananda Yoga Centers also offer four-week Yoga Teachers' Training Courses at their ashrams around the world. More than 6,000 teachers have been trained by Swami Vishnu-devananda and his disciples. For further information call 800-783-9642.

Yogi Bhajan

Ravi Singh, Director of the Kundalini Yoga Center in New York City, tells me that kundalini yoga originated as a house-holder's tradition in North India, specifically designed for busy people who didn't have hours to devote to yoga each day, but who wanted a concentrated and effective practice. Originally it was a closely guarded science reserved for advanced lay students. The code of silence was broken in 1969 when Yogi Bhajan first brought the practice to the United States and began training kundalini yoga teachers. "He felt that at this onset of the Aquarian Age there should be no more secret practices, and he let the cat out of the bag.

"Kundalini is the basic bioenergy of being, the highest frequency of prana. Most people access only enough of this to be barely alive. Kundalini yoga is a systematic and graceful way of building up this energy, a slow catharsis. There are a number of checks and balances built into the process as we work with the nervous and glandular systems to prepare a person to accommodate more energy. If you do the system the way it's taught, you never access more energy than you can gracefully deal with. We don't believe in being overwhelmed. Most of the bad experiences people report are really reflective of their state of blockage rather than their state of openness. Kundalini is the flowering of one's potential, and its awakening should be a positive experience. It's what yoga is directed toward.

"In my classes we always start by warming up the spine with a number of spinal flexes or twists. We put a lot of emphasis on working with the sciatic nerve, so we do a number of pose and counterpose stretches. After the stretching we do a specific sequence. One day we might do a set for the liver, one day we might do a set to open the heart, one day we might do a set for the lungs, one day we might do a set for overcoming fear or anger. In the course of a month everything gets covered.

"We put a lot of emphasis on the breath. We also use a lot of movement. Some people don't get anything from holding poses, but when they move and breathe the benefits are immediate. We're also thinking a mantra along with the breath, so every class is like a moving meditation. And there's a lot of emphasis on the science of sequence and how the exercises work with one another to generate an effect greater than the sum of the parts."

Yogi Bhajan's world-wide organization is called the 3HO Foundation (for Healthy, Happy, Holy). You can call 3HO International Headquarters at 310-552-3416 for the center nearest you. New Yorkers can reach Ravi Singh at 212-475-0212.

Screening Teachers

After numerous phone calls, I had the sense I'd only scratched the surface of the many types of Hatha yoga classes available in the United States today. Still, this synopsis may give you a general feeling for what's out there — what the different attitudes and styles of some of the prominent schools are.

As you think about which Hatha class you'd like to sign up for, I'd encourage you to phone the teacher and ask a few specific questions to guide you in making your decision. Most Hatha instructors are happy to respond to inquiries and to guide you to another tradition if they're not offering what you're looking for. There are two important questions you should be asking when you screen a prospective Hatha teacher. You may well have more.

1. "By which yoga organization are you certified?" Although some excellent teachers are not certified, it's still a good idea to check the teacher's credentials. Students can injure themselves in a Hatha class if their teacher doesn't understand how to assume and hold a posture properly, and how to communicate this process to students. Certification usually means the teacher has had at least rudimentary training in anatomy and physiology, which is imperative if a class is to be taught safely. If you are pregnant, extremely stiff, or have a medical problem such as high blood pressure, mention this to the teacher and make sure she or he knows how to deal with it.

2. "Is your style of teaching gentle, vigorous, or somewhere in between?" It is important to know how physically demanding the class will be. If you are out of shape or have a physical difficulty, like a vertebral disc that tends to slip out of alignment, you may want to start with a slow, relaxed style of Hatha. If on the other hand you're in excellent condition and crave fast-moving, demanding, aerobic workouts, choose a teacher who can accommodate you.

And when you find the Hatha class that's right for you, have a good time!

Linda Johnsen is author of Daughters of the Goddess: The Women Saints of India, *and* The Living Goddess of India.

Reprinted with the permission of YOGA INTERNATIONAL, RR 1, Box 407, Honesdale, PA 18431, 717-253-4929.

Yoga International publishes an annual guide to yoga teachers and classes. To receive this guide free of charge, call Yoga International at 800-584-6999.

A P P E N D I X   D

How To Find The Right Hatha Yoga Teacher

by Sandra Anderson

So you're looking for a yoga teacher. Hatha yoga has become so popular in the past decade good teachers are relatively plentiful in all but the smallest towns. But how do you find the one that's right for you?

Begin with a few minutes of reflection: what do you want from your yoga practice and what do you expect from your teacher? Most of us have many goals and expectations, some of which are outside of our awareness or at best, vaguely defined. But having one or more major goals in mind will help. For instance, if you are seeking relief from a particular problem such as lower back pain, headaches, or curvature of the spine, it may help to ask prospective teachers about their experience and skill in working with that problem. If you want stress relief, you may want a teacher who emphasizes breathing, relaxation techniques, and meditation. If your first priority is strength and flexibility, you may want a more vigorous workout.

- Don't be afraid to ask teachers about their qualifications, their philosophy of yoga, and their teaching style. Good teachers welcome these questions and the answers may tell you immediately whether or not you're interested.

- Choose someone who is well trained—Hatha yoga is not learned from books or videos, and good teachers, regardless of their background or school of yoga, will acknowledge their teacher(s) and will be dedicated to some form of ongoing study and practice. Be wary of anyone who claims to be self-taught.

- Try out a few classes with different teachers and see what works for you. If you're new to the practice of Hatha yoga, it may take some time to settle on a teaching style that you prefer. Even when you have, you will probably find that your needs change with time. Once you attain some strength and flexibility, for example, you may find yourself drawn to a teacher who encourages you to use these attainments to deepen your inner awareness. A fruitful Hatha yoga practice is dynamic—it expands and changes as your capacity increases.

- Be practical in choosing a teacher or yoga center. If you aren't motivated enough to drive an hour across town during rush hour to take a class, choose one that's more convenient. The benefit is in the practice, and no amount of good intentions will make up for it.

- Be kind to yourself. Yoga should be challenging but it should also be enjoyable. If you feel out of place or overwhelmed in a class, keep looking. A good teacher will leave you feeling calm, inspired, and more in touch with yourself. You should look forward to class and enjoy yourself while you are there, even though it stretched you a bit emotionally as well as physically. Respect your feelings.

Which brings us to the last and perhaps the most important question. Does the teacher inspire respect from you? Would you want to be like the teacher? Are you confident she or he can help you reach your goals? Better yet, you may suddenly realize you have bigger dreams than you realized when you started. When you find the right teacher, you'll consider each class a gift you don't want to pass up.

Reprinted with the permission of YOGA INTERNATIONAL, RR 1, Box 407, Honesdale, PA 18431, 717-253-4929.

BIBLIOGRAPHY

CHAPTER TWO: Westerners Search
for the Magic and Mystery of Tibet

Avedon, John F. *In Exile from the Land of Snows*. New York: Alfred A. Knopf, 1984.

Barborka, Geoffrey A. *H. P. Blavatsky, Tibet and Tulku*. Adyar, (India): The Theosophical Publishing House, 1966.

Batchelor, Stephen. *The Tibet Guide*. London: Wisdom Publications, 1987.

Bernbaum, Edwin. *The Way to Shambhala*. Los Angeles: Jeremy P. Tarcher, 1989.

Cranston, Sylvia. *H. P. B. The Extraordinary Life & Influence of Helena Blavatsky, Founder of the Modern Theosophical Movement*. New York: Jeremy P. Tarcher/G. P. Putnam's Sons, 1993.

Das, Surya. *The Snow Lion's Turquoise Mane: Wisdom Tales from Tibet*. San Francisco: Harper San Francisco, 1992.

David-Neel, Alexandra. *Magic and Mystery in Tibet*. New York: Dover Publications, 1971.

David-Neel, Alexandra. *Initiations and Initiates in Tibet*. New York: Dover Publications, 1993.

David-Neel, Alexandra. *My Journey to Lhasa*. Boston: Beacon Press, 1993.

Dowman, Keith. *Masters of Mahamudra: Songs and Histories of the Eighty-Four Buddhist Siddhas.* Albany: State University of New York Press, 1985.

Dowman, Keith. *Masters of Enchantment: The Lives and Legends of the Mahasiddhas.* Rochester, VT: Inner Traditions, 1988.

Evans-Wentz, W. Y. *Tibetan Yoga and Secret Doctrines.* New York: Oxford University Press, 1967.

Foster, Barbara and Michael. *Forbidden Journey: The Life of Alexandra David-Neel.* San Francisco: Harper & Row, 1987.

Gold, Peter. *Altar of the Earth: The Life, Land, and Spirit of Tibet.* Ithaca, NY: Snow Lion, 1987.

Gyaltsen, Shardza Tashi. *Heart Drops of Dharmakaya: Dzogchen Practice of the Bon Tradition.* Translation and commentary by Lopon Tenzin Namdak. Ithaca, NY: Snow Lion, 1993.

Hopkirk, Peter. *Trespassers on the Roof of the World.* Los Angeles: Jeremy P. Tarcher, 1982.

Illion, Theodore. *In Secret Tibet.* Stelle, IL: Adventures Unlimited Press, 1991.

Middleton, Ruth. *Alexandra David-Neel: Portrait of an Adventurer.* Boston: Shambhala Publications, 1989.

Norbu, Namkhai. *Dream Yoga and the Practice of Natural Light.* Edited by Michael Katz. Ithaca, NY: Snow Lion, 1992.

Norbu, Namkhai. *The Crystal and the Way of Light: Sutra, Tantra, and Dzogchen.* Edited by John Shane. New York: Routledge & Kegan Paul International, 1986.

Roerich, Nicholas. *Shambhala: In Search of the New Era.* Rochester, VT: Inner Traditions, 1990.

Roerich, Nicholas. *Heart of Asia: Memoirs from the Himalayas.* Rochester, VT: Inner Traditions, 1990.

Spalding, Baird T. *The Life & Teaching of the Masters of the Far East, Vol. 1.* Marina del Rey, CA: Devorss & Co., 1924.

Spalding, Baird T. *The Life & Teaching of the Masters of the Far East, Vol. 3.* Marina del Rey, CA: Devorss & Co., 1935.

Spalding, Baird T. *The Life & Teaching of the Masters of the Far East, Vol. 5.* Marina del Rey, CA: Devorss & Co., 1955.

Thomas, Lowell, Jr. *Out of This World: Across the Himalayas to Forbidden Tibet.* Garden City, NY: Garden City Books, 1950.

Thurman, Robert A. F., translator. *The Tibetan Book of the Dead.* New York: Bantam Books, 1993.

CHAPTER FOUR: Energy Secrets of the Five Rites

Aivanhov, Omraam Mikhael. *Man's Subtle Bodies and Centres.* Frejus Cedex (France): Editions Prosveta, 1987.

Beinfield, Harriet and Efrem Korngold. *Between Heaven and Earth: A Guide to Chinese Medicine.* New York: Ballantine Books, 1991.

Burr, Harold Saxton. *Blueprint for Immortality: The Electric Patterns of Life.* Saffron Walden, UK: C. W. Daniel, 1972.

Chia, Mantak, with Michael Winn. *Taoist Secrets of Love: Cultivating Male Sexual Energy.* New York: Aurora Press, 1984.

Chopra, Deepak, M.D. *Ageless Body, Timeless Mind: The Quantum Alternative to Growing Old.* New York: Harmony Books, 1993.

Chopra, Deepak, M.D. *Unconditional Life: Mastering the Forces that Shape Personal Reality.* New York: Bantam Books, 1991.

Chu, Valentin. *The Yin-Yang Butterfly: Ancient Chinese Sexual Secrets for Western Lovers.* New York: G. P. Putnam's Sons, 1993.

Cleary, Thomas, translator. *The Secret of the Golden Flower.* San Francisco: Harper San Francisco, 1991.

Clifford, Terry. *Tibetan Buddhist Medicine and Psychiatry: The Diamond Healing.* York Beach, ME: Samuel Weiser, 1984.

Cooper, J.C. *Chinese Alchemy: The Taoist Quest for Immortality.* New York: Sterling Publishing, 1990.

Eisenberg, David, M.D. *Encounters with Qi: Exploring Chinese Medicine.* New York: Penguin Books, 1985.

Firebrace, Peter. *Acupuncture, Restoring the Body's Natural Healing Energy.* New York: Harmony Books, 1988.

Frantzis, Bruce Kumar. *Opening the Energy Gates of Your Body.* Berkeley, CA: North Atlantic Books, 1993.

Gerber, Richard, M.D. *Vibrational Medicine: New Choices for Healing Ourselves.* Santa Fe, NM: Bear & Company, 1988.

Kaptchuk, Ted J., O.M.D. *The Web That Has No Weaver: Understanding Chinese Medicine.* New York: Congdon & Weed, 1983.

Karagulla, Shafica, M.D., and Dora van Gelder Kunz. *The Chakras and the Human Energy Fields.* Wheaton, IL: Theosophical Publishing House, 1989.

Leadbeater, C.W. *The Chakras.* Wheaton, IL: Theosophical Publishing House, 1927.

Liu, Da. *Taoist Health Exercise Book.* New York: Paragon House, 1991.

Mann, Felix. *Acupuncture: The Ancient Chinese Art of Healing and How It Works Scientifically.* New York: Vintage Books, 1973.

Ming-Dao, Deng. *The Wandering Taoist.* San Francisco: Harper & Row, 1983.

Motoyama, Hiroshi. *Theories of the Chakras: Bridge to Higher Consciousness.* Wheaton, IL: Theosophical Publishing House, 1981.

Nan, Huai-Chi. *Tao & Longevity: Mind-Body Transformation.* Translated by Wen Kuan Chu. York Beach, ME: Samuel Weiser, 1984.

Page, Michael. *The Power of Ch'i: An Introduction to Chinese Mysticism & Philosophy.* Wellingborough, UK: The Aquarian Press/Thorsons, 1988.

Sharamon, Shalila and Bodo J. Baginski. *The Chakra Handbook.* Wilmot, WI: Lotus Light Publications, 1991.

CHAPTER SIX: Food Combining and Other Dietary Advice

Bass, Dr. Stanley S. and Chet Day. *Ideal Health Through Sequential Eating.* Winter Haven, FL: Health & Beyond Press, 1994.

Bass, Dr. Stanley S. and Chet Day. *In Search of the Ultimate Diet.* Winter Haven, FL: Health & Beyond Press, 1994.

Bernard, Dr. Neal. *Food for Life.* New York: Harmony Books, 1993.

Day, Chet. *You're Killing Yourself When You Don't Have To: A Natural Hygiene Primer.* Winter Haven, FL: Health & Beyond Press, 1994.

Diamond, Harvey and Marilyn. *Fit for Life.* New York: Warner Books, 1985.

Diamond, Harvey and Marilyn. *Fit for Life II.* New York: Warner Books, 1987.

McDougall, Dr. John. *The McDougall Plan for Superhealth and Life-Long Weight Loss.* Orange, CA: New Century Publishers, 1983.

Ornish, Dr. Dean. *Dr. Dean Ornish's Program for Reversing Heart Disease.* New York: Random House, 1990.

CHAPTER SEVEN: Energetics of the Voice, Sound, and Meditation

Berendt, Joachim-Ernst. *Nada Brahma, The World is Sound — Music and the Landscape of Consciousness*. Rochester, VT: Destiny Books, 1987.

Goldman, Jonathan. *Healing Sounds: The Power of Harmonics*. Rockport, MA: Element Books, 1992.

Govinda, Lama Anagarika. *Creative Meditation and Multi-Dimensional Consciousness*. London: Mandala/George Allen & Unwin, 1977.

Govinda, Lama Anagarika. *Fountains of Tibetan Mysticism*. York Beach, ME: Samuel Weiser, 1969.

Johari, Harish. *Chakras: Energy Centers of Transformation*. Rochester, VT: Destiny Books, 1987.

Johari, Harish. *Sounds of the Chakras* (tape cassette). Rochester, VT: Destiny Recordings, Inner Traditions International, 1990.

Judith, Anodea. *Wheels of Life: A User's Guide to the Chakra System*. St. Paul, MN: Llewellyn Publications, 1990.

Judith, Anodea and Selene Vega. *The Sevenfold Journey: Reclaiming Mind, Body & Spirit Through the Chakras*. Freedom, CA: The Crossing Press, 1993.

Keyes, Laurel Elizabeth. *Toning: The Creative Power of the Voice*. Marina Del Rey, CA: Devorss & Co., 1973.

Schwartz, Howard. *Miriam's Tambourine: Jewish Folktales from Around the World*. New York: Oxford University Press, 1988.

Steiner, Rudolf. *Eurythmy as Visible Speech*. London: Rudolf Steiner Press, 1984.

APPENDIX C

Coleman, Graham, editor. *A Handbook of Tibetan Culture: Guide to Tibetan Centers and Resources Throughout the World.* Boston: Shambhala Publications, 1994.

Goodman, Michael Harris. *The Last Dalai Lama.* Boston: Shambhala Publications, 1987.

Govinda, Lama Anagarika. *The Way of the White Clouds: A Buddhist Pilgrim in Tibet.* Berkeley, CA: Shambhala, 1971.

Gyatso, Tenzin, the 14th Dalai Lama. *Freedom in Exile: The Autobiography of the Dalai Lama.* New York: Harper Collins, 1990.

INDEX